John Payne Collier

Mr. J. Payne Colliers Reply to Mr. N.E.S.A. Hamiltons

John Payne Collier

Mr. J. Payne Colliers Reply to Mr. N.E.S.A. Hamiltons

ISBN/EAN: 9783337071271

Printed in Europe, USA, Canada, Australia, Japan

Cover: Foto ©ninafisch / pixelio.de

More available books at **www.hansebooks.com**

MR. J. PAYNE COLLIER'S REPLY

To MR. N. E. S. A. HAMILTON'S

"INQUIRY" INTO THE

IMPUTED SHAKESPEARE FORGERIES.

LONDON:

BELL AND DALDY, 186 FLEET STREET.

1860.

My Letter in the *Athenæum* of the 18th Feb. last was necessarily written on the spur of the moment, and it will not surprise the reader that it should have stood in some need of correction : the corrections, with additional matter, chiefly in the shape of documents, are supplied in the following pages. Here and there a few' new circumstances have since occurred to my memory ; and these I have also inserted, as well as enlarged others. It ought to be borne in mind that the most recent transaction referred to is now more than ten years old, and that others go back to the distance of twenty, thirty, and thirty-five years : it will not be surprising, therefore, if I have accidentally omitted even particulars which might be important.

REPLY,

&c.

THE substance of what here appears in more detail was published in the *Athenæum* of the 18th ult.; but the charges against me have been got up with such elaborate pomp and circumstance by the Manuscript Department of the British Museum, of which Mr. N. E. S. A. Hamilton is the mouthpiece, and have been printed in so imposing a shape, that I have thought it necessary to give my "Reply" in something like a corresponding form of permanence and prominence, in order, as the question must unavoidably survive the mere interest of the day, that one publication may accompany the other, and that the bane and the antidote may be taken together.

I can have no right to complain that, if there be fair and reasonable ground for believing that a fraud and imposture has been attempted or committed, one department, or even all the departments, of our great national institution should step forward to guard the public against the delusion. I look upon it, in fact, as part of their duty; but they are bound to discharge that duty with as much expedition as is compatible with a proper sifting of the case; and they are bound, moreover, not only to limit themselves, in the execution of their task, to what necessity may require, but to proceed with due regard to the character and dignity of their own position. A dispassionate sobriety ought to be observed, if merely for the sake of the effect to be produced; and the whole inquiry ought to be conducted with the utmost temper and moderation. Above all, no personal animosity or individual antipathy ought to be indulged, much less to be apparent. A spirit of judicial impartiality ought to pervade the proceedings of those who take upon themselves at once to accuse, to investigate, to give evidence, and to decide.

This is a truism so obvious that I shall not endeavour so much to enforce it, as to contrast it with the course the Manuscript Department of the British Museum have adopted in reference to the charges they have brought against me.

In the very beginning of July last, they opened their attacks by the boldest accusations of forgery, confessedly long before they were in possession of evidence to support them: all was then mere assertion; but they promised, without more delay than could not be avoided, to produce their authorities: they should, they said, "shortly lay before the public" all the particulars they could collect. What was the result? They have occupied nearly eight months in their inquiries: in the meantime, if they were believed, I have had to sustain all the odium produced by their preliminary denunciation; and yet, when their matured imputations are brought forward in the shape of an ambitious pamphlet of 155 quarto pages, they are not found to contain even as much as their original statement.*

In the interval, however, they have been far from idle in other ways; they have carried back their researches not merely to the year 1849, when I bought the corrected folio, 1632, of Shakespeare's Works (which, for brevity's sake, I shall call the Perkins folio) of Rodd the bookseller, but even to the year 1823, when, in fact, my avowed career of authorship was only in its commencement. They have hunted in every dirty hole and obscure corner for information; and if they happened to light upon anything that, in their opinion, at all contributed to the end of blackening my character, individual and literary, they have not failed, during the whole of the last seven or eight months, to make it public, not only by paragraphs and articles in newspapers,† but by

---

* Independently of documents and other reprinted matter, there are not 50 pages of the 155 that are new. The composition of these 50 pages occupied more than 220 days, or at the rate of considerably less than a quarter of a page per day—this, too, supposing only one hand to have been employed upon the work ; whereas it is notorious that the Manuscript Department not only brought all their resources to bear on the subject, but called in the aid of the Mineral Department also. We do not here take into account the separate labours of the lithographer. Is this, I may ask, to be taken as a test of the rate at which business is conducted in the Department ? I always thought, and had some reason to think, that it was one of the most industrious and well-conducted departments in the British Museum.

† I wish to avoid giving personal offence, and therefore mention no names ; but it is generally stated that the Manuscript Authorities of the British Museum specially invited gentlemen to see the book, and to listen to their criticisms upon it, who were engaged in various departments of the public press. The name of one gentleman in particular, for whom otherwise I enter-

laboured attacks upon me in magazines and reviews carefully forwarded to me anonymously. No chance was neglected of discovering something to confirm the impression which the Manuscript Department hoped they had produced by their earliest onslaught in *The Times* of the 2nd of July last.*

Surely it will not be said that such a course is creditable to the Manuscript Department of the British Museum, which ought only to be interested in the discovery of truth, for the sake of truth itself, and not for the purpose of injuring private reputation; yet its junior officers, it is said, have from time to time employed themselves in stimulating the public appetite, and in whetting the edge of public curiosity, for the sake, not only of directing

tain a high respect in his own branch of knowledge, has almost invariably been coupled in paragraphs directed against me and my literary labours. While I had any influences of the same kind, as all my friends and relations knew, I studiously kept my own name from thus attracting public attention.

* It is to be observed that at that date they had had the Perkins folio, by consent of his Grace the Duke of Devonshire, for nearly two months in their hands. I have always striven to make myself as unobjectionable as I could, but even my small reputation in an inferior department of letters seems to have excited envy; and I foresaw that, when Lord Campbell, as a kind compliment to that reputation rather than to my merits, addressed to me his letter *On the Legal Acquirements of Shakespeare,* it would materially tend to exasperate my enemies. It had not long been published before Sir F. Madden (who, in September, had intimated to me his wish to see the book) wrote to the Duke of Devonshire in order to borrow the Perkins folio; and having procured it, Mr. N. E. S. A. Hamilton "seized the opportunity," as he himself expressed it, of subjecting it, with the aid of Sir F. Madden and others, to the most rigorous examination.

renewed attention to Mr. N. E. S. A. Hamilton's promised pamphlet, but for the purpose of increasing the prejudice against me.*

The whole of this inquiry and discussion has arisen out of my purchase in 1849 of the Perkins folio, from the late Thomas Rodd, a bookseller whom I had known for at least forty years, and who during the whole of that time carried on a most respectable business in Newport Street, Leicester Square. I have told the story of my acquisition of it so often that, as I am weary of it, and perhaps as the particulars are contained in both editions of my *Notes and Emendations*, and are more than touched upon in my Shakespeare, 6 vols. 8vo. 1858, it may not be necessary to say more on the present occasion than

* Let me here, with the utmost brevity, advert to Mr. T. J. Arnold's articles, two dozen pages long, in *Fraser's Magazine* for January and February, so well-timed as just to precede Mr. N. E. S. A. Hamilton's work. Mr. T. J. Arnold does not, it is true, belong to the MS. Department of the British Museum, but he takes the very same line of argument, uses almost the same expressions as Mr. N. E. S. A. Hamilton, and affords internal evidence of the closest connexion. The reader may remark also the most unfair manner in which an attempt is there made to connect me with a disreputable paper called *The Freebooter*, not merely as a correspondent, but actually as the editor of the publication in which an improper use was once made of my name, and for which the real editor afterwards endeavoured to make amends. I was no more editor than Sir F. Madden, or indeed than Mr. N. E. S. A. Hamilton, who was probably not then born. The transaction occurred so long ago, 1823, that it had quite escaped my memory; but I think I can say with certainty that I never saw more than one number of *The Freebooter*. The whole matter was explained to the late Sir H. Nicolas, and to Mr. Pickering, his publisher. If Mr. T. J. Arnold be the son of the late S. J. Arnold the dramatist, perhaps I can understand part of the cause of his undeserved animosity towards me. It may be an entirely different, but not an indifferent person.

that the Perkins folio came out of a parcel of books
from the country; that I was in Rodd's shop when
the parcel arrived ; that I bought it for thirty
shillings (neither Rodd nor myself being aware of
the existence of any manuscript notes in it); and
that I left it for a time in the shop.* The truth of
this statement has been impugned; and if it have
not been openly and broadly asserted, it has been
more than insinuated that the volume had no notes
whatever when it came into my hands; that I subsequently added them, and that having so inserted
them in an old handwriting, or in what was meant
to look like it, I palmed upon the world my own
alterations and emendations of the text of Shakespeare, as the work of some person who had lived
about the middle of the seventeenth century.

Now, the first answer (besides my own direct
and flat contradiction) I shall make to this charge is
the following note to me from the distinguished
Principal of New Inn Hall, Oxford.

* An unworthy cavil has been raised because in the Preface
to my *Notes and Emendations* I said I " took the book home,"
and in my letter in the *Athenæum* that I " left the volume to be
sent home." The fact, I believe, is that I did *take* the Perkins
folio home, and that it was not *sent* home, but that I left it for a
short time in the shop. My frequent course was to call at Rodd's
on my way from Kensington, to see what he might have that was
new and interesting to me, and if the book or books I had bought
were of any size, to go on towards the City, and on my return to
carry away my purchase by an omnibus. I did not ordinarily
give Rodd the trouble of sending all the way to my house. Such
I feel pretty sure was the case with the Perkins folio: I left it in
the shop until my return, and then I " took it home" with another
folio. My enemies must be hard pressed to rely on such a paltry
quibble as this, or indeed to put it forward at all, as a reason for
doubting the veracity of my statement. I did not sufficiently
speak " by the card."

Dr. Henry Wellesley happened to hear (as who could avoid hearing ?) in July last the imputations cast upon me and my conduct by Mr. Hamilton, and feeling certain that he had seen the Perkins folio, *in its annotated state,* in Rodd's shop, before the volume arrived at my house, he said so to a mutual friend, who communicated the fact to me. Dr. Wellesley must have entered the shop just after I quitted it, and there saw the book in question. He examined it more than Rodd, or I had done,* saw, to use his own words, " an abundance of manuscript notes in the margins," and wished to become the purchaser of the volume; but Rodd told Dr. Wellesley that it was already sold to a customer (probably naming me), and the Principal therefore looked at it no farther. Learning that Dr. Wellesley had so spoken of the transaction, I took the liberty of writing to him, although personally unknown, and of requesting such particulars as he could readily furnish, impressing upon him their importance to me, in order to repel the calumnies with which I had been assailed. I was very soon favoured with the following reply, which in every respect tallied, not merely with what I had heard, but with what I had myself seen :—

" Woodmancote Rectory, Hurstpierpoint,
" August 13th, 1859.

" Sir,

" Although I do not recollect the precise date, I remember some years ago being in the shop of Thomas Rodd on one occasion when *a case of books from the country had just been opened.* One of those books was *an imperfect folio*

---

* Perhaps by a better light. The front shop, where the parcel had been opened by Rodd, was dark from the books in the window, but the back shop was lighted by a large sky-light.

*Shakspeare, with an abundance of manuscript notes in the mar-
gins.* He observed to me that it was of little value to col-
lectors as a copy, *and that the price was thirty shillings.* I
should have taken it myself; but, as he stated that he had put
it by for another customer, I did not continue to examine it;
nor did I think any more about it, until I heard afterwards
that it had been found to possess *great literary curiosity and
value.* In all probability, Mr. Rodd named you to me; but
whether he or others did so, the affair was generally spoken of
at the time, and I never heard it doubted that you had become
the possessor of the book.

" I am, Sir,

" Your faithful and obedient Servant,
" H. WELLESLEY."

"To J. P. Collier, Esq,"

Dr. Wellesley, therefore, saw the Perkins folio,
with " an abundance of manuscript notes in the
margins," in 1849, for Rodd died in that year; and
it remained long in my possession before I became
acquainted with its " great literary curiosity and
value." As soon as I knew it, I proclaimed it without reserve everywhere. I wrote several letters on
the subject in the *Athenæum:* I laid it before a
Council of the Shakespeare Society, specially sum-
moned for the purpose, which was attended by nearly
all the members: I also produced it at the general
meeting of the Society. Besides showing it at two,
if not three, evening meetings of the Society of Antiquaries, I published a letter stating that it would
be upon their library-table for four hours by daylight,
when everybody interested was invited to inspect it.*

* Preface to Collier's Shakespeare, 1858, p. xi. It was not
perhaps convenient to Mr. Hamilton to notice this *daylight* ex-
hibition at all, as there mentioned; nor does he say that the
Perkins folio was shown first at a Council of the Shakespeare
Society, and afterwards at the general meeting of the members.

I did not see there any of the officers of the Manuscript Department of the British Museum ; but I do not know what more I could have done to secure their attention to the book, unless I had carried it to them and begged them to look at it, and to afford it the sanction of their judgment. I have been told, but I do not believe it, that Sir F. Madden and his colleagues were irritated by this piece of supposed neglect ; and that they also took it ill that I presented the Perkins folio to the kindest, most condescending, and most liberal of noblemen,* instead of giving it to their institution. When I placed it in the hands of the Duke of Devonshire, I knew that, for any literary purpose, it would be just as accessible, and just as safe, in his Grace's library, as in that of the British Museum.

I shall make no other remarks in connexion with the preceding note from Dr. Wellesley than that, notwithstanding the lapse of more than ten years since the transaction, it agrees most precisely with my narrative in the Prefaces to the two impressions of my *Notes and Emendations* in 1853 : " the case of books from the country," the " abundance of manuscript notes in the margins," the very price of " thirty shillings " which I had paid for it, and the fact that, according to the Principal's belief, the book

---

* The Duke of Devonshire had the highest reverence for any degree of literary merit, and he was never tired of depreciating his own rank, and elevating that of men of learning and talents. He would not hesitate to show me infinitely more kind attention, than on any score I could lay claim to : as a trifling instance, I may be allowed to mention that, when I was at work in the library at the time he took lunch, he never failed to bring me, with his own hands, a glass of sherry and a biscuit from the ante-room where he sat. Neither was there in this condescension the slightest ostentation of humility.

had devolved into my hands : all these facts show that it could have been no other than the Perkins folio. I consider myself most fortunate to have thus secured such unimpeachable testimony : Dr. Wellesley might have died in the interval between 1849 and 1859 ; or I might myself have expired, and left my memory to be blotted by such unscrupulous adversaries as have recently assailed me. I can never enough thank Dr. Wellesley for the manner in which he has come forward, in the face of all the denunciations of the British Museum against me.

Thus I am warranted in asserting, as I do in the most unqualified manner, that when the volume came into my house it contained all the manuscript alterations for which credit has been given to it by me. Their real date and origin is another question ; and not long after the publication of the first edition of my *Notes and Emendations*, I was led firmly to believe that I could establish that they were in existence early in the present, if not late in the last, century. My book had been out only a short time before I was favoured by the receipt of the following letter by post :—

" Hyde Park Gate, Kensington,
" 25th April, 1853.

" Sir,

" You will, I trust, forgive one who has not the honour of knowing you, for intruding on your leisure, when I state that the subject on which I am about to trouble you is the copy of the folio 1632 of *Shakespeare*, with the MS. emendations, which you have lately given to the world, and for which every lover of Shakspeare is so deeply indebted to you.

" The information which I wish to give you may, if followed up, enable you to trace the ownership of that copy for at least a century back.

" A friend of mine, Mr. Parry, with whom I was lately conversing on your extraordinary and interesting discovery, told me *he many years ago possessed a copy of* THE FOLIO 1632 *which had marginal notes in manuscript,* and which, being in bad order, he never consulted. This copy he lost, he did not know how, and gave himself no concern about it.

" When I showed him the fac-simile of the page out of *Henry VI.,* which forms the frontispiece to your work, Mr. Parry told me *he had no doubt that the copy was the same* as that which he lost, *as he remembered very well the hand-writing, and the state of preservation.* I pressed him to give me all particulars about the work, and how it came into his possession. He told me that *it was given him, with many old books, by an uncle of the name of Grey,* WHO WAS A LITERARY MAN, AND FOND OF CURIOUS WORKS. Mr. Parry believes that Mr. Grey got the copy at the sale of the Perkins library; and all I could learn of these Perkins's is, that they were related to Pope's Arabella Fermor, and that all the family were dead when the sale of their library took place. I urged Mr. Parry to inform you of these circumstances, thinking that they might interest you greatly, and hoping that if you could once trace the copy into the hands of one of the name of Perkins upwards, it might be a clue to further discovery. Whether from indolence or from modesty, Mr. Parry, I find, has not communicated with you; and I therefore told him that I assuredly would, as every fragment of information on such a subject had its value.

" Trusting to your indulgence, and your zeal for our great poet, to excuse the liberty I have taken, believe me to be, sir, ¦

"Your faithful and obedient Servant,
"JOHN CARRICK MOORE.

"J. Payne Collier, Esq."

I knew that Mr. J. Carrick Moore was the nephew of the gallant General, Sir John Moore, who fell before Corunna in 1809, and I need not say how strong a feeling of interest and expectation his zealous note excited in me. I wrote to Mr. Parry, Mr. J. C. Moore having favoured me with his address, but received no answer, owing to a fall Mr. Parry had just suffered. I waited for about ten days, when I ventured to call upon Mr. Moore, who told me of Mr. Parry's accident, and advised me to see him at his residence at St. John's Wood. I did so; and, without repeating what I printed and reprinted in my Prefaces, I may observe that Mr. Parry entirely confirmed every part of Mr. J. C. Moore's communication. He described his uncle, Mr. Grey, *as a man fond of old books, and as having a turn for literature,** and perfectly recollected the appearance of the folio 1632, both inside and outside, *especially dwelling on its rough calf-binding*. He was strong in his belief that the book had come out of the library of a Roman Catholic family of the name of Perkins, residing at Ufton Court, Berkshire; and he added, that an old priest had there shown him, some fifty years before, the empty shelves that had once been filled with the books.

Mr. Parry was so distinct and positive, and so sure as to the identity of the hand-writing in the notes, &c., that I returned home quite convinced that I had certain information as to the existence of those notes in the Perkins folio, at the end of the last or in the beginning of the present century. I was then living in the house of my brother-in-law, about three miles from Maidenhead, and I made an

---

* Such, it will be observed, was Mr. Parry's statement to Mr. J. C. Moore and to myself; yet in a letter from him, published by Mr. Hamilton in *The Times* of August 1, 1859, Mr. Parry observes, "I may also add, that I certainly did not tell, and could not have told, Mr. Collier, that *Mr. Gray was partial to the collection of old books*, for I believe he set no value at all upon them." Mr. Parry's memory is obviously here defective, for he had told Mr. J. C. Moore that his, Mr. Parry's, "*uncle was a literary man and fond of curious works.*"

expedition to Reading, in order to institute some inquiries regarding Ufton Court and the Perkins family. I did not succeed in obtaining any additional information of the slightest importance; but I was fortunate enough to meet with some old books, which had very possibly come out of the Perkins library, two being imperfect tracts by Robert Greene, the celebrated Elizabethan pamphleteer, and the other a copy of Spenser, dated 1611, which had once been the property of Michael Drayton.*

My Preface to the second edition of *Notes and Emendations* was nearly completed when I first heard of Mr. Parry's ancient ownership of the Perkins folio. I finished it upon the strength of Mr. Parry's personal assurances ; and although the press was kept waiting, I carried that Preface with me to St. John's Wood, in order to be quite sure that what I said accorded entirely with Mr. Parry's recollection and statement. I feel no doubt whatever that I then added in that preface the parenthesis

---

* The conduct of the Museum authorities on this question would make people almost afraid of owning that they have on their shelves any books of value with contemporaneous notes ; but I have been all my long life collecting such relics, and I could with ease enumerate several that belong to me, for some of which, in my sanguine days, I gave high prices. I have Chapman's *Twelve Books of Homer's Iliad*, with his autograph inscription at the back of the title to Sir Henry Crofts, and manuscript emendations in various places. I have also the same old poet's *Hymns of Homer*, with a long autograph dedication ; I have Ben Jonson's copy of B. Yong's translation from *Montemayor*, 1598 ; Daniel's copy of his *Poems*, 1602, inscribed to Lady Pembroke ; the Earl of Essex's copy of Drayton's *Pastorals*, 1593, with many valuable corrections, &c. Drayton's copy of Spenser's *Poems*, folio 1611, has also corrections, but whether by Drayton, I have not yet been able absolutely to decide. I have made use of them in the edition of Spenser I am now printing.

that his uncle, Mr. George Grey, "*was partial to the collection of old books,*" at Mr. Parry's express instance; and I remember the words the better, because they tallied so precisely with what was stated in Mr. J. Carrick Moore's letter, and, above all, rendered it so probable, that Mr. Grey had once been the owner of the Perkins folio.

I was in haste to get my Preface to the printer, and I did not, on that occasion, carry the volume itself to St. John's Wood with me; but I afterwards did so, and met Mr. Parry a short distance from his house, walking lame, and aided by a stick. Mr. Parry has since said that he was "using *sticks;*" but this is a slight mistake, which Mr. Hamilton has, possibly only by error, exaggerated into *crutches,* —a word employed by nobody. Mr. Parry was walking with *a* stick; and after expressing my regret at his recent accident, and stating that I had the Perkins folio under my arm, I said that, under the circumstances, I could not think of asking him to return home in order to examine it : he replied, "If you will let me see it now, I shall be able to state at once, whether it was ever my book." I therefore produced it to him on the spot, and held his stick while he looked at the book in several places, including the cover : he then returned it to me with these words, "That was my book; it is the same, but it has been much ill-used since it was in my possession." I then gave him back his stick, and, thanking him for his most satisfactory assurance, I wished him good morning.

Very soon after reaching home, that is to say, within a day or two, it occurred to me that I ought to record Mr. Parry's expressions, and I did so with a pencil at the foot of page iv. of my Preface to the second edition of *Notes and Emendations*, in these words, which, it will be observed, differ from those above used, by having " This " for *That*, and " mis-used " for *ill-used*, but the meaning is of course ex-actly the same.

" I afterwards showed him [*i. e.* Mr. Parry] the book itself, and having looked at it in several places, he said, ' *This was my book : it is the same; but it has been much misused since it was in my posses-sion.' "

Therefore, I can be more certain of nothing than that I exhibited the Perkins folio to Mr. Parry, and that he employed the words regarding it I have im-puted to him. In his letter in *The Times* of August 1, 1859, he observes, "I cannot remember that Mr. Collier ever showed me the book, but I well remem-ber his showing me the fac-simile." Here are at once two mistakes of memory. I most assuredly did show him the book, and as assuredly I did not show him the fac-simile; for Mr. J. Carrick Moore, as he himself states in his letter to me, " showed him the fac-simile of the page out of Henry VI.," when Mr. Parry had "*no doubt that the copy was the same* " as the volume he had owned many years before. Mr. Parry, in his letter in *The Times*, only says that he " *cannot remember :*" he does not say positively that I did not show the book to him, merely that his memory does not serve him upon the point ; mine does serve me most distinctly, that he not only saw the book, but that he turned over several of its leaves, looked at the outside, and then replaced it in my hands. I put the fact on record very soon after the transaction. My evidence is clear and affirmative, while that of Mr. Parry is indistinct and negative.

I do not impute the slightest blame to Mr. Parry. I am confident that he does not mean to deceive or misstate: I merely assert that his memory is defective on this point. I only wish that it were as good as mine; and then I should have no difficulty in establishing that *the Perkins folio of 1632*, with its emendations (the peculiar hand-writing of which Mr. Parry told Mr. J. C. Moore he at once recognised) had been the property of Mr. Parry early in the commencement of the present century.

I have no personal acquaintance with Mr. Parry beyond what I have seen of him in connexion with the book in question; but I believe him to be a man of honour and probity, and he is known to individuals for whom I have the highest respect and esteem. He is, like myself, advanced in years, and certainly little able to compete with the imposing authorities at the British Museum. When he went there on 14th July last, for the purpose of inspecting the Perkins folio, in the presence of Sir F. Madden, Mr. Hamilton, Mr. Maskelyne, and others, he may easily have been confused by the rapid passing and re-passing of the folios of 1623 and 1632 before his eyes; and at last he may not have been able to remember which edition had really been his own book, although he had first told Mr. J. C. Moore, and afterwards myself repeatedly, that *his corrected copy had been the edition of* 1632. The figures 1623 and 1632 are precisely the same, only with an inversion, which may have added to Mr. Parry's confusion;* but I should not be disposed to criticise too

* This is the more probable, because, in one of Mr. T. J.

nicely what may have passed on the occasion at the Museum, because I am sure, whatever he said, that Mr. Parry had no intention to state what was untrue. He spoke to the best of his memory, but his memory was bad ; and he may have been, as it were, cajoled out of his own conviction.

Without Mr. Parry's evidence, which, however, under all the circumstances, I am far from relinquishing (and without having since attempted to see him and to reconvert him to his old opinion, that the Perkins folio of 1632, *and no other*, had been his long before I bought it) I am able to prove conclusively by the Rev. Dr. Wellesley's ready and welcome assistance, that when I purchased the book of Rodd for thirty shillings, out of a parcel just received from the country, it contained "an abundance of manuscript notes in the margins."

These manuscript notes I never altered, added to, nor diminished. How much they may have been altered or diminished, while the Perkins folio was in the hands of the officers of the British Museum, it is impossible for me to judge ; but, I apprehend, on the showing of my antagonists, that something has been obliterated, with or without the consent of the present noble owner of the book. Mr. Maskelyne, before the Duke of Devonshire was applied to for permission, talks of having tested the ink by his tongue, which ink "evidently yielded to the action of damp :" therefore, a portion of the writing may have been thus removed, which was valuable as an

Arnold's papers in *Fraser's Magazine,* he makes a similar blunder, viz., 1853 for 1835 : he represents me as having published my *New Facts* only as long since as 1853, whereas they came out nearly twenty years earlier, in 1835.

emendation, or with reference even to the question of authenticity. How many pages or parts of pages may have been licked over, and licked out, by the tongues of the officers and under-officers of the Manuscript Department, it is impossible for me now to ascertain. Those who may make the same experiment with the book in future will not have a very agreeable duty.

Mr. Maskelyne also cannot deny that some of the writing, which he charges as artificial, has been made with "ordinary ink," or with "a mixture containing ordinary ink;" and who shall say, in the course of the many years that this book must have been more or less under the hands of the corrector, (perhaps in circumstances of difficulty with which we are not at all acquainted,) what inks he may, so long ago, have been under the accidental compulsion of employing? I know that such has not unfrequently been the case with notes I have from time to time made in my own books, especially in a copy of *England's Parnassus*, 1600, on which I have been engaged for the last twenty-five years in supplying the names of authors and their works. I have even sometimes resorted in the first instance to pencil, and when next I had a pen and ink at hand, I have written in ink over my own pencillings. Such a course is surely not unnatural, and therefore, I apprehend, not unusual.

That I did so in the case of the Perkins folio I utterly and absolutely deny; yet that is the impression which has been endeavoured to be produced against me. But, if it be true that pencils of plumbago were at that time in common use, as I believe they were, the old corrector may himself have now and then adopted this mode of *recording on the spot* changes which, in his judgment, ought hereafter permanently to be made in Shakespeare's text. Mr. Hamilton speaks of the bold modern character of the words still to be traced in pencil; but for how much of this boldness and modernness (which for my own part I do not perceive) may we not be indebted to the unconscious lithographer who, under such watchful instructions, made the single fac-simile with which we are favoured.* In his letter in *The Times* of July 2d, 1859, Mr. Hamilton told us that there are an " infinite number " of these pencil-marks; yet his lithograph presents us with *only fifteen* of that "infinite number," and those fifteen relate to the most trifling and insignificant matters. Such specks and atoms as he has construed into letters, and even into words, might have been made in thousands, even during the time the Perkins folio was in the custody of the Manuscript Department. I certainly do not mean to say that this unworthy trick has been played : I am bound here to acquit my adversaries of such paltry and discreditable frauds : what I mean to say is, that if such specks and spots of plumbago be made, there is no word in our

---

* Without meaning at all to imply that it was so, is it not possible that even in giving these instructions, and pointing out to the lithographer the real, or supposed, course of the old pencil-marks, especially if it were done with the point of a pencil, some atoms of *new plumbago* may have found their way to the paper of the Perkins folio, and have been, on all hands, innocently mistaken for *old plumbago?* If the real or supposed course were pointed out with a dry pen, may we not imagine that the dry pen itself might easily make some suspicious indentation on the soft paper of the old book ? I am told that both pencil and dry pen were at times used for the purpose ; and that where plumbago was not to be found in the Perkins folio, indentation was relied upon.

language to which, with the smallest ingenuity, they may not be adapted.* Supposing, however, that such a word as "begging" (one of Mr. Hamilton's illustrations) were ever so plain in the Perkins folio, what is gained by it? There is actually no corresponding emendation of the old printed copy, so that "begging" must have been written in the margin, not as a suggestion for a change of language, but merely as an explanation, and a bad explanation too, if it refer to "pregnant" in the poet's text. No man who pretends to understand Shakespeare would

---

* On this point and some others I may be allowed to borrow the following note from the *Athenæum* of the 25th Feb. It comes from the most trustworthy and experienced lithographer in Europe, whose opinion is constantly sought and relied upon in our courts of justice :—

"113 St. Martin's Lane, February 22.

"Seeing in the *Athenæum* of last Saturday that my name has been used both by Mr. Collier, and also in your critique on Mr. Hamilton's ' Inquiry,' &c., and, as the general reader may suppose I have been engaged by both parties, permit me to state, that not myself, but my son, F. G. Netherclift, who is separated from me and in business alone, was employed by the party at the British Museum on the fac-similes in Mr. Hamilton's pamphlet. I had no knowledge of it or part in it, nor, under the circumstances, would I have attempted to show pencil-marks over or under any ink writing by any mode of printing ; whilst, from my knowledge of facts, and my high respect for the character of Mr. Collier, for whom I have made very numerous fac-similes in the course of the last thirty years, I could not have joined in any way to aid this causeless and cruel persecution against him. As I am continually *subpœnaed* in the Law Courts to give evidence in matters relating to handwriting, and some kind cross-examining counsel may make a 'mare's nest' of the above circumstance, may I request the favour of your inserting this letter in the *Athenæum?*

"I remain, &c.,
"Joseph Netherclift, Sen."

think of placing "begging" in the margin as the true sense of "pregnant."

Is it not strange, if pencil-marks can be pointed out, as supposed instructions for such words, and fragments of words, as Mr. Hamilton has given us, that not the smallest trace of pencil is to be found in connexion with the entire lines, sentences, and parts of sentences, which abound in the Perkins folio? There the old corrector has left *ex confesso* no vestige of a mark. Mr. Hamilton does not pretend to have found one atom of plumbago there, and, if it had been to be found, the powerful microscope which he and his coadjutors employed could not have failed to detect it.* Supposing for an instant,—I only suppose it—that anybody had maliciously and surreptitiously introduced these specks and

---

* In my letter in the *Athenæum* of the 18th Feb., I committed an error when I applied the terms *Simonides Uranius* to a microscope. I have no pretensions to science of any kind, and I misunderstood Mr. Maskelyne's parenthesis. I correct my own blunder here (which no doubt many others have already set right), because, irrelevant as it is, even that might in some way, for aught I know, be tortured into proof of fraud. It is just as much so as the twenty odd pages Mr. N. E. S. A. Hamilton has filled with real or supposed omissions in *Hamlet*, many of which I never dreamed at any time of including. How does it prove forgery if it could be shown that I had carelessly left out of my emendations all the proposed changes in *Hamlet?* The authorities of the Manuscript Department are no great logicians, or they would have been sensible that the emphasis they lay on the emendations in *Hamlet* is an unwilling tribute to their importance, if not to their excellence. The same remark will apply to Mr. Hamilton's ostentatious display of the few manuscript emendations in the Bridgewater folio, 1623, of which, by the way, *he himself omits two.* The fact is that few things are more difficult than to be utterly faultless in such extracts. I spared no pains to be accurate, but how often may the eye be deceived in turning over 900 folio pages in double columns, full of minor, as well as of major alterations.

spots for the purpose of discrediting the ink emendations, it would have been very easy to have applied
them as hints for a lithographer in forming such
short words as "wall," "now," or "over" (which
Mr. Hamilton has relied upon), but impossible to
have annexed them to whole lines and sentences
without their being observed in an instant, and followed by the naked eye. For instance, if the two
substituted lines in *Hamlet*, Act V., had been first
entirely written in pencil, and then inserted in ink,
the pencil could have been traced, more or less,
through the whole course of the couplet; it would not
have been a mere dot or touch, and nothing besides.

I declare most positively, in the face of the whole
world, that, while the Perkins folio was in my hands,
I never saw a pencil-mark in it that I had not made
myself, either as a note of reference to some other
book, or as a point of observation connected with the
book itself. If I wanted to be sure not to forget to
look at a particular passage in *Malone*, or in any
other commentator, or if I wished to note something
that required again to be examined in the folio, I
took the ordinary method with a pencil that I always
kept at hand ; but that I thus added the slightest
hint with reference to any projected alteration of the
language of the poet I deny in the strongest form in
which it is possible to clothe a denial. If a fancy
should ever cross the mind of any one who has ever
seen me write, that such and such a word or letter
in Mr. Hamilton's lithograph is not unlike my hand,
I can only say that for the last fifty years my hand-
writing must have been familiar to many in the
British Museum; and that if the likeness have been
more than merely accidental, the fact has an origin

not much to the credit of our national establishment. I do not impute it:* I only assert that no letter, syllable, or word of *so-called* bold and modern writing in Mr. Hamilton's fac-simile was placed in the Perkins folio by me. I never saw Mr. Hamilton's writing, but he must, from his position, often have have seen mine, and I will venture to say, that his lithograph of supposed pencil-words is quite as like his hand as mine.

It may be urged that my eyes are bad, even when aided by spectacles; that the late Duke of Devonshire's eyes (though about two years younger than my own) were also bad; but it is a fact that, neither together nor separately, did we ever discover a single pencil-mark. I exhibited the Perkins folio by candle-light and by day-light, and it was turned about in every possible direction by those who inspected it, and I never yet heard of an individual who saw pencil-marks, until after the volume had been deposited in

---

* Other people, however, may not be so charitable. I lent the book for a week to a very intimate and most intelligent Shakespearian friend in my own neighbourhood, who writes me a note containing the following supposed address to Mr. Hamilton and his coadjutors :—" Gentlemen of the Manuscript Department, who impute fraud and forgery to Mr. Collier, what could you reply to any one who declared his suspicion, that, to serve your turn, *you had fabricated the pencillings* on the side of the old corrector's notes and emendations?" My friend goes on to assert that, " in the whole week that the Perkins folio was every day under his eyes, when *he examined every page of it, he never saw a single pencil-mark,* nor any indication which would lead him to doubt the *bona fides* of the whole body of the emendations." He doubted many of them as a matter of criticism, but never doubted that they were genuine. Surely, if pencil-marks were required, as instructions for the subsequent insertion of trifling expletives, they would be doubly necessary for long, new passages, so confessedly Shakespearian.

the Manuscript Department of the British Museum : there, according to Mr. Hamilton, an " infinite number" were discovered. Even now I defy him to show any such "infinite number ;" and it is not immaterial to mention that the able and most pains-taking lithographer I employed never saw one of them. Mr. Netherclift, senior, had the book in his hands, while it was still mine, several times, and for an indefinite period ; for he and his assistants not only executed the fac-simile which accompanied both editions of my *Notes and Emendations*, but *eighteen other facsimiles from as many different parts of the volume*, which were privately made for me, as the severest tests of the genuineness and importance of the emendations. Yet he assures me, in a letter now before me, that he and his assistants never once discovered a pencil-mark from the first page to the last, excepting my avowed pencillings and lines round the passages I wished to be imitated. I placed my book unreservedly in his hands, with no other charge than to take care of it : he might show it to whom he pleased ; and, if he had doubted, he would have done me a favour to have asked any competent authority.

All I maintain is that the pencil-marks are so few, so small, and so indistinct, that it is only by the exercise of the most tortuous ingenuity that they can be transformed into words and letters ; and that if they were brought before any intelligent and well-educated jury, as proofs, not merely of mine, but of Mr. Hamilton's, or of any other man's hand-writing, the case would at once be scouted out of every court of justice in the empire.

. I am tired of this subject of pencillings : but there is one observation upon them, growing out of

Mr. Maskelyne's Letter in *The Times*, dated 13th July, 1859, which I must be allowed to make. He is mysteriously great upon the question, whether in some places the pencil overlies the ink, or the ink the pencil, apparently forgetting that if the pencil-mark overlies the ink, the pencil-mark must have been made last: he admits, however, without reserve, that *"in several places the pencil stops abruptly at the ink."* Is not this decisive? Why does it "stop abruptly at the ink," but because the ink had been previously written, and the person who made the pencil-mark went no farther than the ink would allow him? Truly, all this discussion about "the lustre of the plumbago," and about the plumbago "just traceable under the ink," is too paltry and puerile for a man of Mr. Maskelyne's scientific attainments; and it almost makes one smile to read his grave and authoritative denunciation of the *u* in *Richard II.*, and of the "tick" which "intersects each limb of that letter." If, as he tells us, the pencil sometimes *stops at the ink*, there is an end of the question, as far as every word so circumstanced is concerned.

And now let me ask, what has become of the wonderful binding-discovery which Mr. Hamilton declared in his Letter in *The Times* of 2d July, 1859, that he had made? He says not one syllable about it in the body of his pamphlet, but in his appendix (p. 133) he has thrust in a note, which does not at all explain away his original contradiction, when he first called the binding, as I myself had done in my Prefaces, "rough calf;" and afterwards, "rough sheep." Besides, a mighty fuss was made in his first letter regarding the water-mark on the fly-leaf. I dispute neither the "rough sheep" nor the water-mark. It is no part of my case to do so; for I expressly said in my Prefaces to *Notes and Emendations*, 1853, that it was not even the second coat the Perkins folio had worn. The fly-leaf, with its "G. R. and Dutch Lion," so exultingly dwelt upon by Mr. Hamilton, may easily have been inserted even later; but, later or earlier, *it has been abstracted from the book;* and when it came from the Manuscript Department, no fly-leaf was found in it. I do not deny the "G. R." nor the "Dutch Lion;" but, for aught that appears, all this was a pure invention by Mr. Hamilton. He, or somebody else, has deprived us of the means of testing his assertion: as his "calf" has been metamorphosed into a "sheep," so his "G. R." may by this time have been turned into C. R., and his "Dutch Lion" into an English one. Hence, possibly, the present absence of the fly-leaf.

How and why the Manuscript authorities of the British Museum have been heated into such animosity towards me I cannot pretend to explain. I was always upon good terms with Sir F. Madden, whom I have known for more than a quarter of a century, and upon two occasions I was of some service to him. Of one of them I can say no more; but of the other I may remark that it occurred within the last two or three years, and it was when he had involved himself in an awkward scrape by purchasing manuscripts, which he ought to have known had been dishonestly come by. They had in some way escaped from Lord Ellesmere's Collection, and the most obvious and important of them had actually been printed in a volume, with which Sir F. Madden ought to have been well acquainted. The late Earl Ellesmere heard of the strange circumstance, put the matter into the hands of his solicitor, and asked me to inquire of Sir F. Madden as to the facts. I did so; and finding, as I of course expected, that Sir F. Madden had innocently, though ignorantly and most incautiously, become possessed of the documents, they were restored to the noble owner, and the matter was dropped. Sir F. Madden showed me some of the manuscripts he had thus purchased, possibly all. One of them was an entire volume relating to the Mint in the reign of Elizabeth, with the handwriting of Sir Thomas Egerton (afterwards Lord Chancellor and Baron Ellesmere) on nearly every page, which Sir F. Madden, with his great skill and experience in palæography, might have recognised; and the other was a very remarkable document on parchment— so remarkable, that it is astonishing how Sir F. Madden could have become possessed of it without suspicion. It was an Address from all the Members of Lincoln's Inn to the Queen in 1584, declaring that they would defend her to the last against Spain, and against all her open or concealed enemies ; and the very first name at the bottom of the instrument (and it contained very many) was that of Sir Thomas Egerton, then Solicitor-General. This document was printed at full length in the *Egerton Papers* by the Camden Society in 1840, and when it was printed it attracted much attention. Nevertheless, Sir F. Madden had bought the original ; and the late Earl of Ellesmere wished the matter to be investigated, though, as far as I am aware, it was never his design to prosecute. Really and truly, if Sir F. Madden had then been indicted for receiving stolen goods, knowing them to have been stolen, it might have gone hard with him.   I should willingly have been one of his witnesses to character.

Some men can forget an injury who never can forgive an obligation; but I assure Sir F. Madden that he was not in the slightest degree indebted to me on the occasion: all along the Earl of Ellesmere was convinced that the Keeper of the Manuscripts had only acted carelessly, not criminally. The crime indeed lay elsewhere.   Therefore I cannot for a moment suppose that Sir F. Madden and the younger officers of his department have taken any antipathy to me on this score.   If the late Earl of Ellesmere, and my always kind and bountiful patron, and I may call him friend, the late Duke of Devonshire, had any ultimate design of placing me in a distinguished, but invidious position in the British Museum, which design secured me enemies there, I can only say that I never heard of it from either.   They wished me well, I am certain; but whether they attempted and failed in doing well for me in this respect, I cannot decide.   I heard of it, it is true, but not from them.   When the highest office in that great national establishment was, not very long since, vacant, I was urged to send in my name as a candidate for the place; but I was not only well acquainted with the feebleness of my own claims, but with the strength of the interest, and the greatness of the abilities, that were opposed to me.

If the Duke and Earl had succeeded in any such project, I could hardly have experienced more bitter hostility than has been displayed towards me in my merely private capacity, as a writer of many productions tending to the illustration of our native language, and of the great authors who have employed it. The earliest work I published on the subject was in 1820, but I had previously written various anonymous essays and articles; and I was called to the Bar too late in life to have a chance of success against younger competitors. I therefore devoted myself mainly to letters, occupying all my spare time in a way that was sufficiently remunerative, but extremely fatiguing, generally keeping me up so late at night that I seldom got to bed until others were rising. My time and pen were thus fully occupied; and I never had the leisure, even if I had possessed the inclination, to devote myself to the writing and acquisition of feigned hands of any period, much less to the extremely difficult task of imitating the writing of two or three centuries ago. The general reader must here take my word for it, but I have not a relation or friend who does not know that in every way I was *incapable* of it. Here the charge is, not only that I acquired one, but many ancient hands — that I manufactured public and private documents at will; and, beyond all, that I filled the Perkins folio with thousands of emendations and corrections, besides altering the old and incorrect punctuation in an incalculable number of instances.

There is one point that my antagonists, in their eagerness to convict me, have entirely forgotten : indeed I apprehend that they are hardly qualified to form a judgment upon the literary excellence of not a few of the alterations suggested in the margins of the Perkins folio. Their vision is only not microscopic when they look back ten, twenty, thirty, and even forty years into the incidents of my long life, and fancy that with telescopic

power they behold me sitting with manufactured
inks in a close and obscure study, and hard at work
upon old-seeming fabrications. They have left no
stone unturned, in the hope of finding a poisonous
toad under it—no place unsearched for some dirty
and neglected imputation; but as to the faculty of
judging of what is good or bad in criticism — of
what is excellent or mistaken in illustration, or of
what is valuable or worthless as a wide question
of composition and poetry—they prudently do not
pretend to it. These are points to which the manuscript authorities do not affect to be competent; but
whatever can be done by microscope, and even by a
more powerful moral magnifier, they eagerly " seize
the opportunity" to undertake; or if upon such
matters they hesitate, they call for the aid of other
departments. Then, indeed, the distorted monstro-
sities in an atom of plumbago are equalled only by
the magnified horrors of a drop of Thames water.

These gentlemen forget, therefore, that the indisputable emendations of the Perkins folio, which have
called forth the admiration even of the most bigoted
and antiquated editors, must be assigned to somebody. If I forged them, the least they can do is
to give me credit for them; and I can only say that
I would fain accept them upon any other terms
than that of having been their fabricator. Only
make out for me a legal and legitimate paternity,
and I will adopt the numerous and well-looking
family with joy and gratitude.

The fact, however, is, as almost everybody who
knows me can bear witness, that I have never
enjoyed facilities absolutely necessary to such elaborate trickery. I have not only wanted time and

skill, but place and means. I was married forty-four years ago, and in five out of the eight houses I have since occupied I never had a study to myself: my dwellings were too small and my family too large to allow of it. The common eating-room was therefore my common writing-room, liable to all sorts of interruptions, through which, by long habit, I continued my occupations; and if it were possible to accumulate into one point of view all that my pen then produced, by day and by night, people would be astonished at the mass of writing which, by the exercise of unwonted mental energy and power of abstraction, I was able to accomplish. I was always a hard-working man, and often was called upon to perform tasks I would fain have avoided. When I have had a study, I defy the world to show that I ever turned the key to prevent intrusion: everybody was admitted, and at all hours. Such impositions as are charged against me could not be attempted without seclusion and secresy; yet I had no secrets: my wife opened every letter I received; and in my study was always kept a chest of drawers to which every member of the family had access 'for some of the most ordinary requirements.*

Therefore upon nobody could this charge of fraud and forgery against me have come with greater astonishment than upon my children: if my wife had lived, I believe, it would have killed her to have known that such a base accusation had been

---

* I cannot forbear quoting here a brief passage from the letter of an old friend of eighty-four, now residing in the west of England, who, many years since, called upon me for a literary purpose. He is speaking of my "Reply," as it appeared in the *Athenæum* of 18th Feb.: — "The paragraph in your letter

kept hanging over her husband's head for eight
months, when she was well aware that it could be
refuted in about as many minutes.

I really have not patience, and, well as I can
usually command my feelings, I fear not temper, to
enter in detail into a discussion of Mr. Hamilton's
supplemental and subsidiary imputations, all of them
trumped up with the view to giving some appearance
of plausibility to the accusation, that I am myself the
author of the pen and pencil emendations in the
Perkins folio.

I admit, without reserve, that the weakest part of
my case relates to the finding of Shakespeare documents among the late Earl of Ellesmere's MSS. at
Bridgewater House. And why is it the weakest part
of my case ? For this sole reason, that I never could
have had any direct corroboration of my own testimony as to the discovery of them : nobody was with
me at the precise moment, although the noble owner
of the papers had been in the room only a few
minutes before. Mr. Hamilton, boldly begging the
whole question, styles them " the Bridgewater Shakespeare Forgeries." They may be "forgeries," but
at that time it never entered my head that they could
be so ; and at that time I had never heard the fact,
since mentioned, that Steevens had formerly been
admitted into the rooms which held both the books
and manuscripts. I do not believe that he had

alluding to your study and your private mode of life affected
me much, recollecting, as I perfectly do, the room in which you
kindly received me, when I called upon you about *Robin Hood
Ballads.* I well remember that one of your daughters was in the
front part of your parlour, while you retired into the back part to
examine your book-shelves."

any more hand in the "forgeries" than the Rev. H. J. Todd, with whom I once conversed about the papers,* and who had, as I understood, for some years filled the office of Librarian.

I never suspected the papers to be anything but what they purported to be, and the moment I discovered them and had hastily read them over, I carried them to the Earl of Ellesmere (then Lord Francis Leveson Gower) and read them to him. At his Lordship's instance I copied them, and left both originals and copies with his Lordship. Going again to Bridgewater House (I think it must have been on the very next day, for I was all eagerness to pursue my search) I overtook his Lordship about to enter the door, having just alighted from his horse. He told me that he had seen Mr. Murray, the publisher, who offered to give me £50 or £100 (I believe the smaller to have been the sum) if I would put the documents into shape and write an introduction to them. I declined the proposal at once, saying that I could not consent to make money out of his Lordship's property. Lord Ellesmere appeared a little surprised at my hyper-squeamishness, and replied, with his habitual generosity, that the documents were as much mine as his, for though I had found them in his house, but for me, they might never have been discovered till doomsday.

This circumstantiality may surprise some of my

---

* My object was to gain from him some information respecting the MS. where the performance of "Othello" before the Queen at Sir Thomas Egerton's was mentioned. Mr. Todd was very deaf, and I could learn no more from him than that he knew that such a circumstance was mentioned in some MS. In fact, part of the direction of a letter to the Rev. Mr. Todd remained between the leaves to keep the place, when I saw the book.

antagonists, and they may (like Mr. T. J. Arnold in *Fraser's Magazine*) endeavour to turn it against me with a *more suo*, &c. ; but, although twenty-five years have since elapsed, I have the clearest re-collection of the main facts, and I give them as they occurred. From Bridgewater House I took all the papers, originals and transcripts, to Rodd's, the bookseller, where we examined them carefully ; and, although I at first agreed that he should sell some copies of them when printed, I after-wards (upon my own principle, as stated to Lord Ellesmere) altered my resolution, and only a few *New Facts* were passed over Rodd's counter to his customers.

New Facts was therefore privately printed in 1835 at my own expense, and the same was the case with *New Particulars* and *Farther Particulars;* if any copies of these three tracts were sold, it was without my knowledge, and without my advan-tage : I do not believe it, as Rodd was a very conscientious and scrupulous man of business. In-deed, until the appearance of the first edition of my Shakespeare in 1843, I had never received one farthing for anything I had written regarding Shakespeare or his works. Of course, I do not include the few scattered points relating to him and his plays in my *History of English Dramatic Poetry and the Stage.* My *Memoirs of Alleyn*, the *Alleyn Papers*, Gosson's *School of Abuse*, Nash's *Pierce Penniless*, and perhaps other works, were edited for the Shakespeare Society (of which I happened to be Director) before 1843, and it was the principle of that association that nobody should be paid for trouble of that kind. I am confident that I place it much below the amount, when I say that I was £100 positively out of pocket for printing, paper, &c., in illustration of my favourite pursuits.

After the discovery of the Perkins folio, and after I had laid it on the table of the Council of the Shakespeare Society, for the inspection of about twenty gentlemen and scholars, I told them, in all sincerity, that far from wishing to make money by it, I hoped that they would accept from me, as a free gift, a volume of *Notes and Emendations* founded upon it, then in rapid preparation. Time was taken to consider of the matter, and I was afterwards informed that, as the book would certainly secure a considerable sale, the Council were of opinion that it would neither be fair to me, nor to the trade, that the Shakespeare Society should first print it. I yielded (as everybody knows who was present) with some reluctance, and *Notes and Emendations* was afterwards published by Messrs. Whittaker and Co. as a supplemental volume to my Shakespeare of 1843. Part of this information is in some sort necessary to my case, but I should not have said so much about it, if I had not seen a few of the facts detailed in print by the literary newspaper called the *Critic*. It really has only done me justice in the matter; and I thank it, in perfect ignorance, as far as my own knowledge is concerned, of what it may have said about me at other times and on other subjects. Literary newspapers must usually take opposite sides upon questions of the day; and if the *Critic* have been, as I am informed, strongly opposed to me, it is partly, perhaps, because others have been energetic in my favour.

I am not of a money-getting, or of a money-saving turn, as all my friends and relations can witness ; and I am sure that the Duke of Devonshire and the Earl of Ellesmere never thought me unprincipled or mercenary.

For the first I have often laid out large sums, once £1400 in a single month ; and for the last I have frequently bought very expensive books : his Lordship allowed me always to lay out a certain sum per annum for the gradual formation of a Shakespeare Library; and neither the Duke nor the Earl ever expected from me receipt or memorandum.

My brochure, *New Facts regarding the Life of Shakespeare,* was in the form of a letter addressed to my old and constant friend Thomas Amyot, Esq. (not George Amyot, as Mr. Hamilton calls him) for above twenty years Treasurer of the Society of Antiquaries ; who, had he now been living, could have afforded me most essential aid in my defence against the calumnies so industriously got up. My enemies have waited (I do not at all mean purposely) until, as might be expected in a series of scarcely less than forty years, I have been deprived by death of nearly all the witnesses I could have adduced in support of my own testimony. I say nothing of the Duke of Devonshire, because he knew little that was important of his own knowledge ; but the late Earl of Ellesmere could have given most valuable testimony on many points : so with the late Sir Harris Nicolas; my old contemporary Mr. Barron Field; John Allen, Esq., Master of Dulwich College ; the Rev. H. J. Todd ; James Boswell, the nephew of Mr. Malone ; Mr. Lemon, senior ; Mr. Frederick Devon, formerly of the Chapter House ; the Right Hon. J. W. Croker ; Mr. Hallam ; Mr. Thorpe ; and Mr.

Rodd. My late wife and my eldest daughter were always willing helpmates, especially in the collation of proofs, and knew more or less of almost everything of a literary nature that proceeded from my pen. These are all no more, and yet all could have rendered me some degree of assistance in repelling an attack like the present : I am now left almost alone, and write in the country, without the opportunity of even consulting a friend. In the case of the two last, my wife and my eldest · daughter, I can hardly regret that they did not survive to witness the suffering and irritation that, even in my innocence from all just imputation, I have been compelled for many months to endure. The losses I have sustained in friends and relations must in some measure account for any noticeable deficiencies in my narrative.

Besides the manuscripts found at Bridgewater House, which formed the main substance of my *New Facts*, another document (at what date I am uncertain) subsequently turned up in the same collection, which rendered it most probable that the account of the claims of the Players and Proprietors of the Blackfriars' Theatre, on their proposed removal from that precinct, was authentic : Lord Ellesmere insisted that I should keep it, as it was no necessary part of the other documents. It was a sort of summary of the account of the claims, in an Italian hand of the period, and underneath, in the hand-writing of Sir George Buck, the Master of the Revels to James I. was his memorandum that the Players and Proprietors demanded more than their interest was worth by £1500 : he first wrote £2000, but subsequently altered the sum to £1500. We know that the

Blackfriars' Theatre was in use as a private place of dramatic entertainment long afterwards; and it is to be concluded that the treaty for the purchase of it, either by the Crown or by the City of London, was broken off.

The copy of a letter signed H. S. (supposed to represent the initials of Henry Earl of Southampton) has attracted more attention than, perhaps, any of the other documents discovered in the same depository. It introduced, or has been supposed to have introduced, Shakespeare and Burbadge to the first Lord Ellesmere, then Lord Chancellor; but it is not necessary that I should further describe a paper, which has been at least thrice printed by myself, and which has been inserted in every recent Life of our great Dramatist. As it was in my possession, and had been so for some years, I produced it at a meeting of the Council of the Shakespeare Society about the year 1843 or 1844. I forget what individual members were present, but the authenticity of it seemed generally admitted, and I afterwards had a facsimile of it made by Mr. Netherclift, senior.

I put him under no restriction as to showing " the H. S. Letter " to anybody; and when he re-delivered it to me, I asked him his opinion of it, knowing that he had paid great attention to the modes of writing at the period of its supposed date : his answer was in these words, —" If at any time you happen to want a witness that it is a genuine document, I will be that witness." He subsequently (I cannot fix the precise date) lithographed in fac-simile the other documents I discovered at Bridge-water House. A few weeks since I replaced the whole of them in his hands, and, after looking over them, he acknowledged the fac-similes as his own work, and reiterated his opinion that the originals, to the best of his belief, were authentic. A separate sheet of the water-marks of the paper on which they were written was added by Mr. Netherclift, in order that no information on a point, which, from time to time, has led to the exposure of much fraud, might in this case be wanting.

If I had manufactured the " Bridgewater House Shakespeare Forgeries," as Mr. Hamilton is pleased to call them, surely it is not likely that I should have placed them, without the slightest scruple or caution, in such skilful and knowing hands.

Let us see how these fac-similes were received by very capable judges. I sent copies of them to the Rev. Alexander Dyce (then my intimate friend in spite of his self-regretted attack upon me, as an editor of Shakespeare, in his *Remarks*, &c., 1844) but in the first instance only of " the H. S. Letter," for that was lithographed some time before the rest. What was his answer, not sent in haste, but after considerable delay and deliberation ? It was in these very words, which I copy from a note in his own hand-writing : —

" *The fac-simile has certainly removed from my mind all doubts about the genuineness of the letter.*"

This opinion, be it observed, was given while the Rev. A. Dyce was printing his " Beaumont and Fletcher," and before he entertained any immediate project of publishing a Shakespeare. Although I had known him very intimately from the year 1828 to the time I quitted London in 1850, it is remarkable that he never, on a single occasion, intimated to me a doubt as to the authenticity of any of " the Bridge-

water House Shakespeare Forgeries." In his Shakespeare of 1857 I learned, for the first time, that he
reiterated the suspicions some had expressed; and
it was then, be it remembered, that he was actually
engaged on an edition of Shakespeare intended to
rival mine; and it was then that he, for the first
time, threw all sorts of discredit on my discoveries.
As he had formerly given a decided opinion in
favour of the genuineness of "the H. S. Letter,"
surely, when he subsequently, in his Shakespeare,
expressed his doubts, and quoted the doubts of
others, he might have added, that at one time he
had misled Mr. Collier on the subject, by strength-
ening his belief that "the H. S. Letter" was a genuine manuscript of the period. The Rev. A. Dyce
did not pursue this obvious course for his own
reasons, but I doubt how far they are at present
satisfactory even to himself.

If Mr. Halliwell have seen ground to alter his
decision on the same question, I can have no right
to complain : all I know is, that with regard to "the
H.S. Letter," up to the year 1848, he gave it as his
positive conviction, not merely that it was a genuine
manuscript of the period, but that it could hardly (for
a reason he assigned, and which at least convinced
himself) be a forgery. In his *Life of Shakespeare,*
8vo. 1848, after giving a fac-simile of the conclusion
of " the H.S. Letter," p. 225, he observes :— " The
fac-simile of that portion of it relating to Shakespeare, which the reader will find at the commencement of this volume, will suffice *to convince any one
acquainted with such matters that it is a genuine
manuscript of the period.* No forgery of so long a
document *could present so perfect a continuity of*

design; yet it is right to state that grave doubts have been thrown on its authenticity. A portion of the fac-simile will exhibit on examination a peculiarity few suppositious documents would afford, part of the imperfectly formed letter *h*, in the word *Shakespeare*, appearing by a slip of the pen in the letter *f* immediately beneath it."

Mr. Halliwell then refers to Mr. Wright, who also had seen the original, as a highly competent judge of such matters, a point few will dispute; and he subjoins in a note, " In the library of the Society of Antiquaries, No. 201, Art. 3, is preserved ' a copye of the commyssion of Sewers in the countye of Kent,' marked as *vera copia*, and singularly enough, written apparently by the same hand that copied the letter of H.S." As I have never seen this " copy of a commission," I can offer no opinion upon the identity of handwriting, but it is a matter upon which no man can be better qualified to give final judgment than Mr. Halliwell.

Upon opinions such as those I have acted in uniformly attaching the weight and value of authenticity to the documents in question. I may be wrong, or others may be in error; but all the facts within my knowledge are before the world. The documents themselves, after I had printed them, remained for many years in my possession,—at least from 1836 to about 1845 : Lord Ellesmere never asked for them, nor inquired regarding them ; but one day, after 1845, Lord Ellesmere either told me, or wrote to me, that Mr. J. Wilson Croker had questioned their genuineness. His Lordship, therefore, desired me to send the original papers to his house: I did so instantly, and expressed my

satisfaction that he had resumed possession of what
was his own property, though he had kindly permitted
it to remain so long in my custody.   When I saw
Lord Ellesmere next, some weeks had elapsed, and
he informed me that in the interval the documents
had been " tested:" he did not say by whom, nor in
what way; but he added that he was perfectly satis-
fied.   Afterwards Mr. Croker learned that I had,
among my other manuscripts, an original poem by
Pope, as the fact certainly was : he applied to me
for it for his new edition, and I sent it to him,
and he returned it to me with thanks, adding,
that there was no doubt as to Pope's hand-writing.
This introduced the topic of the Ellesmere Shakespeare manuscripts, and he informed me that he was
now a believer in them, after having inspected them.
The late Mr. Hallam at a dinner, while I filled the
office either of Treasurer, or of one of the Vice-
presidents of the Society of Antiquaries, gave me
similar information.*   While, therefore, I freely
acknowledge the finding of those documents, the
forging of them I as firmly deny.

I do not think that the Earl of Ellesmere would,
in 1847, have appointed me Secretary to the Royal
Commission on the British Museum (an office that,
of itself, raised up against me some enemies in that
institution), if his Lordship had not entertained a
sufficiently good opinion of my integrity.

Before I quit Bridgewater House, my adver-

---

* Mr. Hallam, as I always understood, though I never had the
good fortune to hear him say so, was a maintainer of the excellence (and of their genuineness from their excellence) of the
notes and emendations in the Perkins folio.   On this point others
may easily be more capable of speaking than I can profess to be.

saries have made it necessary for me to notice the copy of the folio of Shakespeare's Works in 1623, there preserved : it contains a few manuscript emendations, which I inserted in my first edition, and have transferred to my second. It is made a question, or rather I should say it is broadly asserted, that they are in the same hand-writing as that of the "Bridgewater House Shakespeare Forgeries," and as that of the Perkins folio. I have not seen them for many years ; but my memory strangely fails me if such is the fact : and I think I do not ask too much when I request that Mr. Hamilton's interested testimony should not be implicitly received, while the present Earl's evidence is entirely suppressed. The noble Lord, in a letter to an acquaintance of mine, gives an opinion on the point, of which, he expressly says, I am at liberty to make use: it is in the following words, and I thank his Lordship heartily for the permission :—

" There is *no pretence, whatever*, for saying that the emendations in the Perkins Shakespeare are in the same handwriting as those in my first folio : on the contrary, except as they are (or profess to be) of the same period, *they are quite different*."

If I were to see all three together, *i.e.* the Perkins folio, Lord Ellesmere's folio, 1623, and the Bridgewater House documents, on the same table, and by the same light, considering the general, and even párticular, resemblances of hand-writing at that date, I might have much difficulty in deciding whether this letter or that letter were sufficiently like others in form and manner, as to warrant a positive conclusion. I more than doubt Mr. Hamilton's opportunities for forming any decision. Nothing

could well be more uncertain, even under the most
favourable circumstances for forming a judgment;
but as it never occurred to me to compare any of
them, I must let the matter rest on my general and
distinct asseveration, that, if it be meant that I had a
concern in writing all, any, or either of them, nothing can be more false and unfounded.

I now come to speak of the Manuscripts at
Dulwich College, and how they have been most un-
fairly thrown into the scale, in order that they may
weigh against me with the rest of Mr. N. E. S. A.
Hamilton's accumulation of trash and trumpery.

First of all, it will be expedient for me to quote
a passage from Malone's *Inquiry*, published in 1796;
it is from p. 215.

> We see from hence that Shakspeare had no motive to reside
> in the Blackfriars before this period [March 1604-5]. The
> truth, indeed, I believe, is that he never resided in the Black-
> friars at all.   From a paper *now before me, which formerly
> belonged to Edward Alleyn, the player, our poet appears to have
> lived in Southwark, near the Bear-Garden, in* 1596.   Another
> curious document *in my possession,* which will be produced in
> the History of his Life, affords the strongest presumptive
> evidence *that he continued to reside in Southwark to the
> year* 1608."

Let it be borne in mind that the documents,
which Malone here and elsewhere refers to, were, in
fact, the property of the Master, Warden and
Fellows of Dulwich College — that Malone had
quietly taken possession of them — that they remained in his hands for several years — that he did
exactly what he liked with them — that he cut off
signatures of old dramatists and players to place
them on the title-pages of his own books — and that
he or others mutilated *Henslowe's Diary* in such a

way, that some of the most valuable portions are now entirely lost. Even the books, the title-pages of which he decorated with the old autographs, had belonged to Dulwich College; for he contrived to persuade the Master, Warden and Fellows, of that day, that Old Plays and Old Poetry did not half so well become their shelves, as the musty divinity, dull chronicles, and other volumes of the same sort, which he substituted. Hence the bulk of his collection; and he must have chuckled amazingly at his success in persuading unsuspecting people to make an exchange of works, which would sell for hundreds of pounds, for others not worth as many shillings. So of the Manuscripts: they seem to have allowed Malone to carry away such as he pleased, to keep them as long as he pleased, and to return such as he pleased, in the state which he pleased. Some that he did not return found their way again to their old home after his death; and it is not very long since the College, most properly, bought back a bundle of papers that must have originally come out of its archives.

It was to all that remained, that I had, by the kindness and confidence of the authorities, between about the year 1825 and 1830, access in the first instance, when I was completing my materials for *The History of English Dramatic Poetry and the Stage.* I cannot call to mind the precise date, but I can well recollect the politeness and readiness of the then Master to aid my researches. I had been introduced to him personally by my learned and excellent friend Mr. Amyot.

One of the first documents I looked at was, I think, a letter from Mrs. Alleyn to her husband,

dated 3rd Oct., 1603, upon which has now been
founded the charge that I interpolated a passage not
met with in the original. It was in one place in
so decayed and crumbling a condition from the
effects of damp and time, that I was obliged to
handle it with the utmost caution. I did not read
it nor examine it closely until afterwards, how long
I do not pretend to say, but a friend, now unfortu-
nately dead, was with me, and we then read as
follows, in the latter part of the letter.

" Aboute a weeke a goe came a youthe, who said
he was Mr. Frauncis Chaloner, who would have
borrowed x^{li} to have bought things for * * *, and
said he was known unto you, and Mr. Shakespeare
of the globe, who came * * * said he knewe hym
not, onely he herde of hym that he was a roge, * * *
so he was glade we did not lend him the monney
* * *. Richard Johnes [went] to seeke and inquire
after the fellow, and said he had lent hym a horse.
I feare me he gulled hym, thoughe he gulled not us."
Memoirs of Edward Alleyn, 8vo. 1841, p. 63.

Now the question is, and the only question of the
slightest importance (though that is in truth of little
moment) whether the name of " Mr. Shakespeare of
the globe " occurred in the most rotten and frag-
mentary part of the letter at the time when I copied
it. Whether it did or did not is not of the smallest
interest, as regards the biography of our poet,
especially as there were two, if not three, other
Shakespeares " of the Globe " Theatre, then resident
in Southwark.* However, the charge is that from the

---

* One of these was an Edward Shakespeare, of whom nobody
had ever heard till I published his name in 1846 (*Lives of Shakespeare's Actors*, Introd. p. xv.) from the Registers of Cripplegate

mere love of deception (for I could have no other motive) I imagined the part of the letter in which the name of Shakespeare occurs, and corrupted the immediately adjoining portions for the purpose of giving my invention support.

It is indisputable that since I first saw and copied the letter at Dulwich, portions of it have crumbled away and entirely disappeared; so that Mr. Hamilton's account of the contents differs from mine : he accuses me not only of inaccuracy, but of fraud and wilful misrepresentation. I do not deny that it is possible I misread some utterly unimportant letters or words : the paper was in such a state of demolition that it was extremely difficult to make any sense out of the latter part of it ; but I did my best to give a faithful transcript, and I am absolutely certain that " Mr. Shakespeare of the globe " was spoken of in it, and in the way I stated. Mr. Hamilton asserts that " there is not the smallest trace of authority for any allusion to Shakespeare :" this may be very true ; he is speaking of Mrs. Alleyn's letter in its present condition, but that is not the question : the question is, whether, when I saw the letter, some thirty, or even more years ago, the name of " Mr. Shakespeare of the globe " was not to be traced. I maintain that it was ; and had an intimate and excellent friend been still alive, I could have substantiated it by his evidence as well as by my own. Mr. Hamilton insists that the name of Shakespeare never was to be seen on any part of the paper which is now

Parish. I may here express my wonder that the MS. Department of the British Museum has not contended that I invented and forged most of the particulars I derived especially from the Southwark, Cripplegate, and Shoreditch parochial records.

E

rotted away; but how can he tell whether it did or
did not exist there, when he cannot deny that much
of what was originally written on that part of the
paper has been utterly annihilated? Excepting as
it impeaches me, the whole is really a *lana caprina*
matter, valuable, perhaps, to Mr. Hamilton and to
his coadjutors in the distress of their case, but utterly
worthless to anybody else.

Here allow me to ask this question : If I had
purposely misstated the import and contents of the
letter, adding that it was in a state of ruinous decay,
what would have been the natural course for me to
have pursued? would it not have been to have left
the letter as it was, in the hope that when it was next
seen and consulted, as much of it might have disappeared as possible? Instead of doing so—instead
of leaving it still exposed to the action of air and
accident, I carefully inclosed it in paper, and either
I or my friend wrote on the outside, that within was
a document of value, which should not be roughly
handled. I have also a faint recollection that I
especially directed the attention of the Master of
the College, or of the Librarian, to it : at all events,
I diligently wrapped it up, as if to make sure that
the next person who opened the paper should see
that I had been guilty of fraud. If, indeed, I had so
misrepresented the contents of the crumbling relic,
what was to prevent my rubbing away a little more
of the old paper, and who then would have been able
to detect the trick I had played? I have never, I think,
seen the letter from the day I copied it until this
moment; but I understand that the envelope, on
which my caution was written, is still in existence,
though it did not suit the purpose of my adversaries

to mention the care I had taken, if I were guilty, to preserve the evidence of my guilt.*

Such is the way in which these accusations have been prepared; I will not say manufactured. The passage I have quoted from Malone's *Inquiry*, shows that he knew from the documents before him, that is to say, from documents derived from Dulwich College, that Shakespeare was in all human probability living in Southwark during twelve successive years.

Mrs. Alleyn's letter proves that "Mr. Shakespeare of the globe" was seen in Southwark in October, 1603, and this was doubtless one of Malone's reasons for concluding that our great dramatist had a residence in Southwark from 1596 to 1608.

Malone, nevertheless, was unquestionably in error as to the latter year; for it is certain that it should be 1609; because the assessment to the poor for the liberty of the Clink, in which the names of Shakespeare, Henslowe and Alleyn appear, as giving a weekly contribution of 6*d.*, is dated 8th April, 1609: 1608 ended on 25th March, so that the year 1609

---

* See the *Athenæum* of 25th Feb. last, p. 269. The Editor seems to have been incredulous upon the point whether I did actually leave Mrs. Alleyn's letter so carefully inclosed, but he found it in an envelope inscribed thus: "Important document —not to be handled until bound, and repaired, the lower part being rotten." "Would any man in his senses (asks the Editor) sedulously guard from harm a document which he had consciously misread? Would any rogue guilty of foisting in a paragraph into a public paper, take pains to call instant and incessant attention to the very document which would witness to his crime? No one out of Bedlam." How happens it, I may be allowed to ask, that Mr. N. E. S. A. Hamilton says not one syllable of the pains I had volunteered to take that the letter should not receive farther injury? Does not this trifling fact tend to prove the *animus* with which I am pursued?

had then commenced exactly a fortnight, for which
Malone did not allow. In my letter in the *Athenæum*,
of 18th Feb., 1859, I hastily supposed (writing in a
hurry for immediate publication) that Mr. Hamilton
referred to this assessment: I was mistaken.* There
is no doubt that it was in existence when Malone
published his *Inquiry* in 1796, and that he had seen
it. I was then only seven years old, and of course
merely a probationer in " pothooks and hangers," so
that Mr. Hamilton will hardly contend that at that
early age I could be a proficient in forgery.

The " list of players," which Mr. Hamilton
charges as a modern addition to a genuine document,
I saw and quoted with the other papers ; and if the
names were forged, I can only say that they must
have been upon the instrument when it was seen by
Malone before 1796, although he did not extract it,
reserving it, perhaps, (as I said in my *Memoirs of
Edward Alleyn*) for his *Life of Shakespeare*. My
materials for those *Memoirs* were in great part col-
lected while I was engaged on my *History of English
Dramatic Poetry and the Stage;* and I can most
distinctly aver that the "list of players" was then
extant, and that it was seen by Mr. Amyot, who
accompanied me in one of my earlier expeditions to
Dulwich. I myself state (*Mem. of Alleyn*, p. 67)
that the " list " itself is " in a different hand and in
different ink," which I need not have mentioned,
if I had not wished to produce all the circumstances

---

* The reader will be so good as to observe that I emphatically
acknowledge my error. I call attention to it, lest Mr. Hamilton
should be disposed to argue that I purposely drew attention to one
document, that I might lead people's minds away from another.
My case as to that other is still stronger.

regarding it, that would enable a correct judgment to be formed of its authenticity. Moreover, to set this matter completely at rest, I have now before me Malone's copy of his *Inquiry* (8vo, 1796), as annotated by him for a second edition : it is full of scribbled scraps and notes with information, not contained in the first edition, and on the back of a letter addressed to "Mr. Malone, Queen Anne Street, East," is the very list of players in question. Therefore, whether it were or were not an addition subsequent to the date of the original document to which it is appended, it is certain that it was seen by Malone very many years before I was at Dulwich.*

If any of the documents returned to Dulwich College after Malone's death appear to have been tampered with, I most distinctly acquit him of any such misconduct. Whatever I may be, in the opinion of my adversaries, I feel sure that he was a man of honour and principle ; and supposing, only for a moment, that we were on a par in that respect, it must be admitted that Malone, with all the documents in his private room for years, had infinitely

---

* This book I bought some years after I had printed my *Memoirs of Alleyn* in 1841. As a bibliographical note, and as it may serve hereafter as a means of identifying the book (though Malone's writing, print-like or current, is to be found in hundreds of places in it), I quote the following particulars from the fly-leaf: Mr. Hamilton is fond of fly-leaves and their water-marks, and he may like to know that "1795" is distinctly to be seen in the substance of the paper. Malone's note is this:—"*For a second edition.* Begun to be written about the 10th of January. Begun to be printed about the 20th of January; finished at the press, Monday, March 28: published March 31st, 1796.—500 copies sold on that day and the next." So that it took Malone less than *three months* to write and print an 8vo. vol. of 424 pages.

the advantage over me, as far as the commission of fraud and forgery is concerned. At Dulwich I was never, at that period, anywhere but in a public library-room, always open, not only to the fellows and the servants of the College, but to individuals in the neighbourhood, who were well known. What opportunity I had for committing any of these elaborate offences, my antagonists have not attempted to show : I do not mean to say that I was not often alone, and for some time, but never without the constant danger of being interrupted and detected in my imputed practices.

With reference to the *Player's Challenge*, beginning, " Sweete Nedde, nowe wynne an other wager," which Mr. Hamilton declares a "forgery from beginning to end, although executed with singular dexterity," I may remark that Mr. Halliwell quotes it in his *Life of Shakespeare*, 8vo. 1848, p. 329, after having "collated it with the original ;" and he does not drop the remotest hint that he thought it a forgery. I have no particular recollection of the manner in which it is written, but, contrary to what Mr. Hamilton says, that it is "executed with singular dexterity," it now seems to me that the reduplication of consonants, and other points of orthography in it, might possibly raise suspicion.

What surprises me, in reference to the Dulwich Manuscripts, is that Mr. Hamilton should have confined his objections to such paltry points, when in the course of the *Memoirs of Alleyn*, I have for the first time printed so many papers of importance that are passed by without a word of notice. What does he say, for instance, to Ben Jonson's translation from Martial, to Sir W. Alexander's copy of verses, to Dekker's and Field's Letters, and to nearly the whole of Alleyn's part in R. Greene's *Orlando Furioso*, 1594, with various other curious original documents? All these receive no comment—and with very good reason, I can well believe.

I do not perceive in his *Inquiry* that Mr. Hamilton speaks, as he did in his letters in *The Times* of July last, of paint, pigment, and manufactured inks;* but I know, and he knows, that any ink, however old, may be removed if proper methods be applied; and the scientific department of the British Museum cannot be wanting in skill in this particular. The late Thomas Rodd, the bookseller, undertook for me, and accomplished it, to abolish the slightest appearance of ink-stain from scribbled title-pages; and I myself have taken envelopes sent from different hemispheres, east and west, and have obliterated the addresses by the simplest application. In truth, as most people are aware, no test of the genuine or the spurious can be more uncertain; and if the Trustees of the British Museum would give me leave, I could promise, with no other means, to expunge every vestige of the famous signature, " Willm Shakspere," in the Montaigne's *Essays* by Florio, 1603, for which alone Sir F. Madden paid out of the public purse no less a sum than £130. I am sure that he would not let it stand the test even of a sponge and

---

* In my Prefaces to *Notes and Emendations* I have myself not omitted to state that " the ink in the Perkins folio was of various shades, differing sometimes on the same page," and in the body of the book I have in several places, and with reference to particular emendations, pointed out the same peculiarity. I did so in order to enable people to form a just estimate upon the question of authenticity, as applied to the whole volume; and if I omitted any information of the kind, it was quite unintentionally.

water; and yet Mr. Maskelyne and Mr. Hamilton licked over the Perkins folio *ad libitum*, and were delighted to find that they could manage to get off some of the supposed colouring matter. They do not tell us how much of the soft surface of the old paper they destroyed in this process.

I am now glad to arrive at the last count in the indictment against me; it amounts to the very grave charge, that I was guilty of manufacturing and forging a State paper—a document deposited in the National Archives, and still existing there.

Many years were employed by me in collecting materials for my *History of English Dramatic Poetry and the Stage:* it was published twenty-nine years ago, and I think it took more than a year to print it, for it was a work requiring more accuracy than despatch: it was certainly not ready for press until 1829 or 1830, and it bears date in 1831. I cannot speak positively upon the point, but I think it must be about thirty-three or thirty-four years ago, that I first obtained admission into the State Paper Office that I might copy documents that bore upon my subject.

That always willing and zealous friend, Mr. Amyot, then Treasurer of the Society of Antiquaries, gave me a personal introduction to Mr. Lemon, the father of the gentleman who is now so deservedly high in the Department. Mr. Lemon, senior, was at that date in a post of great trust and confidence, and at my earnest request he promised to look out for me certain muniments relating to plays and theatres. I believe that, as he took a lively interest in my pursuits, he bestowed a good deal of pains on searching out relics that would contribute to my

purpose—and calling in Great George Street, where
the State Papers were then kept before their removal
to their present abode, I found, much to my satisfaction, that he had instituted so active an inquiry,
that he had discovered for me five or six papers of
great novelty and curiosity.

My belief is that the office hours did not extend
beyond three in the day; and as it was late before I
arrived, I expressed my fears that I should not be
able to copy all the documents that morning. One
of them, I well remember, was a Memorial from
some of the principal inhabitants of the precinct of
Blackfriars against the continuance of a theatre there,
on the ground that it was a nuisance,—that it attracted disorderly crowds, and that, as it was about
to be repaired and enlarged by the players, the an-
noyance would be increased. Another document
was in the form of a Petition from the players against
that Memorial ; and this last Mr. Lemon very kindly
undertook either to copy, or to get copied for me:
he took it away for the purpose, and by the time I
had made some extracts from the Memorial, he returned into the room where I was sitting, with the
Petition and the transcript of it in his hand. He
was good enough to aid me in the collation of the
two, and when we had finished, he took away the
Petition itself (which I never saw again, but the
authenticity of which I never for a moment doubted)
and left me the copy, which I used for my book,
sending the very same sheet to the printer of my
History.

My notion was that Mr. Lemon's son, the present
head of the family, had copied the paper for me; but
I have since understood that such was not the case.

Even now, after the lapse of so many years, if it had been of any consequence, I might have been able to decide the point, had I not, when I quitted London in the spring of 1850, for the sake of putting everything into as small a compass as I could, sent away or destroyed all my proof-sheets, and the manuscript belonging to them. Until then it had been my constant habit to tie in bundles the proofs and " copy" of every separate work in which I had been concerned from 1820 to 1850. A large parcel of old, useless letters, shared the same fate, as I could not carry them with me into the country, and as the Pantechnicon would have charged heavily for the space they would have occupied.

That this Petition existed in the State Paper Office before I knew where that office was, is quite clear. It was found for, and pointed out to me, by Mr. Lemon, senior. Mr. Lemon, junior, still in that department, bears witness that *it was known, both to himself and to his father*, before I had been admitted into the State Paper Office : of this fact there exists the best possible evidence ; for the Editor of the *Athenæum*, having learned that such was the case, very récently wrote the subsequent note to Mr. Lemon, making the inquiry whether what he had heard were true :—

"Athenæum Office, Feb. 13, 1860.

" The Editor of the *Athenæum* presents his compliments to Mr. Lemon, and referring to the Petition of the Players— contained in the bundle of papers in the State Paper Office marked ' Bundle No. 222, Elizabeth, 1596,' a copy of which has been printed in text by Mr. Collier, and in fac-simile by Mr. Halliwell, takes the liberty of inquiring whether, within Mr. Lemon's knowledge, that Petition of the Players was in the State Paper Office before Mr. Collier began his researches in that office?   An early answer will oblige."

The inquiry was, of course, very material; not merely with reference to the authenticity of the Petition, but with reference to the impossibility of my being concerned in "the surreptitious introduction of it," to use Mr. Hamilton's words.   The answer, forwarded by return of post, was entirely satisfactory, and in these terms :—

"State Paper Office, Feb. 14, 1860.
"DEAR SIR,
"In reply to your question, I beg to state that the Petition of the Players of the Blackfriars Theatre, alluded to in your note, was well known to my father and myself, before Mr. Payne Collier began his researches in this office. I am pretty confident that my father himself brought it under the notice of Mr. Collier, in whose researches he took great interest.
"I am very faithfully yours,
"R. LEMON.
"The Editor of the Athenæum."

I am not aware, therefore, that it is necessary for me to say more upon this part of the subject.   Mr. Lemon, senior, undoubtedly did bring the Players' Petition under my notice, and very much obliged to him I was, that he took so much trouble to assist me in my literary investigations.   The genuineness of the Memorial, to which the Petition is obviously an answer, has, I believe, not been questioned; and as it is dated 1596, it may be said to ascertain that the Petition, which has no date, was of the same period. The following quotation from the *Loseley Manuscripts* (edited by the late A. J. Kempe, Esq.), 8vo., 1835, p. 496, proves in what way the Players at the

Blackfriars, at about this period, intended to enlarge their theatre, viz. by taking in part of the house of Sir William More.

" Lord Hunsdon to Sir William More. Wishes to take a house of him in the Blackfriars. Hears he has already parted with a portion of his own house to some that mean to make a playhouse of it. So-merset House, Jan. 9, 1595."

At that time, " Jan. 9, 1595," was in fact Jan. 9, 1596, which tallies with the date of the Memorial and consequent Petition. We know besides, that, in May, 1596, it was directed that the Players should not be disturbed. These, however, are only points of history, rendering it probable that the Players did present such a Petition; for it cannot now be disputed that I was not the discoverer of the document, but that having been found by the late Mr. Lemon, he brought it to my knowledge, and kindly procured it to be copied for me, in order to expedite me in my under-taking.

I consider myself much more than fortunate to be able to procure this important and indisputable piece of evidence; for, had the present Mr. Lemon died between about 1828 and 1860, how might not my enemies have triumphed in their imputation, that I had first forged the Petition, and then smuggled it into the State Paper Office!

Of the investigation instituted by the Master of the Rolls, from which Mr. Lemon was apparently excluded, and in which Mr. Hamilton was cer-tainly included (though absolutely an interested party), all I shall say is, that there might be very sufficient reasons for not inviting Mr. Lemon to assist, seeing that *he knew perfectly well that the document in question was in the State Paper Office before I commenced my researches* in that department. Unless I "surreptitiously introduced it" before I knew where the State Paper Office was, even Mr. Hamilton and the Manuscript Department of the British Museum must acquit me of any concern in the supposed fabrication of it.

Have we not here, let me ask, another proof of the sort of spirit by which my adversaries seem to be influenced? While they most indelicately select Mr. N. E. S. A. Hamilton as a coadjutor in the inquiry respecting this Players' Petition, they, as it seems, carefully shut out from that inquiry the very man who could have given them conclusive information. That information, however, would have been fatal to their accusation.

As to Mr. Hamilton's sort of challenge " to produce a remarkable document," so " minutely stated by me " in the *Athenæum*, 6th Dec., 1856, and printed for the first time in my last edition of *Shakespeare*, iii., p. 214, I merely have to remark that it would become Mr. Hamilton, as an officer of the Manuscript Department of the British Museum, to be better informed about our public muniments before he scatters imputations in his usual fashion of *inuendo*. Why does he not say honestly, and at once, that he does not believe in the existence of any " Examination " of Augustine Phillipps, the fellow-actor with Shakespeare?* Perhaps he may be

---

* Let me take this opportunity of correcting a misprint in my copy of that very curious document: for " Sir Charles Pryce" and "Jostlyne Pryce" we must of course read *Sir Charles Percye* and *Jostlyne Percye*. The body of the paper is in Chief Justice Popham's infamously illegible scrawl.

equally incredulous respecting the " Examination " of Sir Gilly Meyricke, which I published in my new *Life of Shakespeare*, 1858, p. 154. These are documents that I found and printed ; but if we were to stay until such interesting papers are discovered by the Manuscript Department of the British Museum, we might wait, I fear, as many years as we have waited months for the recent pamphlet.*

It may even be doubted whether those officers do not owe me some ill-will for finding them work. Only a year or two ago I procured, for a comparative trifle, three large cases of Bentinck manuscripts from Germany, belonging to the period treated by Lord Macaulay in his recent History. How far they illustrate our annals of that time I know not, as I never looked at them ; but being asked by a friend in Oldenburg whither they ought to be sent, I at once recommended the British Museum. These manuscripts may, for aught I know, be yet uncatalogued; I presume not; and such industrious workmen as Mr. N. E. S. A. Hamilton may have suffered in point of labour, from the occupation I was thus the innocent means of procuring for them.

I humbly and earnestly hope that all but my

---

* It is astonishing how little the Keepers and Assistant Keepers in our national depository appear to know of anything that is not immediately under their own eyes. One night, at the Society of Antiquaries, I produced copies of two letters from the famous Richard Hakluyt ; and one of the Museum Assistant Keepers, printing something about them afterwards, was obliged to confess his ignorance as to where the originals were deposited. I also stated that I knew of a copy (now before me while I am writing) of Hakluyt's *Divers Voyages touching America*, 4to. 1582, *with both the maps*. It did not gain credence from the Museum authority, who spoke of the "*supposed* possessor."

impenetrable enemies will be of opinion that I have
cleared myself reasonably well — I put it in no
stronger form — from all fair suspicion of guilt; and
especially from any discreditable connexion with the
emendations in the Perkins folio. The Rev. Dr.
Wellesley knows that they were in it when I bought
the book in 1849. It is all very well for certain
people to decry them : those rival editors who do
decry them, have often been compelled, by the especial
excellence of the proposed changes, to adopt them.
To have only suggested them would have made
the fortune of any man ; and, if I were the real
author of them, what could have induced me *to
foist them into an old folio and to give anybody else
the credit of them?* The charge is so ridiculous
that it carries its own contradiction. Mr. Singer
inserted many with very grudging acknowledgment,
and adopted others, as if they were his own improvements : Mr. Knight behaved in a more straight-
forward way, but availed himself of them. The Rev.
Mr. Dyce has been driven to the hard necessity of
doing nearly the same, with this salvo, that in order
to discredit the Perkins folio he has asserted, un-
knowingly I believe, that some of the best changes
of text were contained in Mr. Singer's corrected folio,
when Mr. Singer never had a corrected folio that presented them, or anything like them. Important as
were other coincidences, it is remarkable that there
never was the smallest outcry for the production
of Mr. Singer's folio, and for the best of all reasons,
—that the production of it would have directly con-
tradicted those who disparaged the Perkins folio.*

---

* I do not think that Mr. Singer ever pretended that the

I know well what it must have cost the Rev. Alexander Dyce to insert such emendations as " diseases" for *degrees*, of " mirror'd " for *married*, of " bollen" for *woollen*, of " bisson multitude " for

emendations in his folio 1632 had any claim to consideration on the score of antiquity : on the contrary, I believe that some minor points, which concurred with those in the Perkins folio, were at one time not to be found in Mr. Singer's folio. I however entirely acquit him of introducing them. I never saw the work by Mr. Singer, called *Shakespeare Vindicated*, but I heard that he spoke hardly of me in it, and I took no notice of his attack : at last he seems to have been won over by his own convictions (for late in life he admitted that he had pursued a wrong system of commentation, if I may use the word) and by my patience, and in 1854 he presented me with a small translation, containing this inscription : " To J. P. Collier, Esq.—with Mr. Singer's compliments — *a peace-offering*." I at once accepted the amicable gift, and wrote him a letter of thanks in the following terms :—

"Maidenhead, 3d March, 1854.

" MY DEAR SIR,

" I am much obliged to you for your interesting little volume (which reached me yesterday) but more for the inscription it contains. I gladly receive it in the spirit in which, I presume, it is intended.

" I know not how far you have advanced in your new edition of Shakespeare, but I heartily wish you success in your endeavours to free his text from corruptions, and to render his meaning intelligible. Such has been the labour of my life, and I shall rejoice if it be the triumph of yours. Allow me to subscribe myself,

" Yours very sincerely,
" J. PAYNE COLLIER.

" S. W. Singer, Esq."

For some reason or other I never received the slightest recognition of my note, unless the series of imputations cast upon me in the course of Mr. Singer's Shakespeare, 12mo. 1856, are to be so considered. What had occurred to counteract his repentant and pacific disposition of the spring of 1854, I never inquired. My earnest wish was to keep on good terms with everybody.

bosom multiplied, and many others ;* but he did insert them after he became an editor of Shakespeare; having before that, while he was yet friendly with me, written under his own hand that not a few of the emendations in the Perkins folio were "*so admirable that they can hardly be conjectural.*" This, too, when my volume of *Notes and Emendations* had been some weeks in his hands, so that he cannot say that he gave a hasty and unconsidered opinion. He must pardon me for once more reminding him of his very words, for they so forcibly

* The two first of these changes of text the Rev. A. Dyce vindicates on the ground that *they are supported by corrections in Mr. Singer's folio,* as well as in the Perkins folio, when the fact is that Mr. Singer's folio has neither of them : indeed, as to the first, Mr. Singer in his *Shakespeare,* v. 179, justifies *degrees* instead of "diseases," and blames those who, with the Perkins folio, have substituted " diseases," not pretending that he has any corrected folio that reads " diseases." As to the second, "mirror'd" for *married* (Singer's *Shakesp.* vii. 242), precisely the same remark will apply, excepting that Mr. Singer had the boldness to print " mirror'd," as if it were his own unprompted emendation, omitting to mention the Perkins folio, and not for an instant urging that he had any authority but his own conjecture for the alteration. Yet both these important changes the Rev. Mr. Dyce assigns to Mr. Singer's corrected folio, as if he wished to deprive the Perkins folio of the sole merit of such great improvements of the text. This, to say the least of it, is very unfair, and I willingly believe that Mr. Dyce unconsciously fell into an error in both cases. As to verbal objections to the Perkins folio, on the ground that modern words are found in its MS. notes, all that it is necessary to say is, that *wheedling,* though used by Butler just after the Restoration, was *pointed out by myself;* and that *cheer* was in use as a word of encouragement and approbation early in the reign of Elizabeth, and that the expression *three cheers* is found in *Teonge's Diary,* from 1675 to 1679. Yet we are told by the enemies of the Perkins folio that the earliest use of *three cheers* was about 1806 ! Those who make such unfounded objections come very ill provided to maintain them.

F

express my own convictions, and indeed almost go beyond them, that I cannot refuse myself the satisfaction of quoting them, whenever an occasion fairly presents itself.

As I stated in the Preface to my *Shakespeare*, 6 vols. 8vo. 1858, I am unable to guess what had operated so hostilely on the mind of the Rev. A. Dyce, beyond the fact, that in 1843 I had anticipated him in his project of publishing an edition of the poet's works. I have never seen even a quotation from his recent attack on my latest labours; but I hear that his anger scarcely knows bounds. I had occasion, in my Preface, to animadvert upon his animosity to me, and upon the mode in which he had treated my labours in 1844, when his adverse *Remarks* almost instantly followed the appearance of my first impression; and in his *Few Notes*, which, in 1853, were specially directed against my volume of *Notes and Emendations*. I heard, incidentally and accidentally, that he was offended at what I had written; and I immediately addressed a mutual friend, stating that my least object was to do injustice to a gentleman and a scholar whom I had known intimately for thirty years: I therefore offered to retract every syllable that was injurious, *if it could be shown to be unjust*, and to make my retractation public in every possible way. Subsequently I found that the Rev. Mr. Dyce was serious in his intention to publish an answer to my Preface; and thinking that a knowledge of my offer to our mutual friend might not have reached him, I wrote to him precisely to the same effect. This note he passed by with entire silence; but I never since have uttered, or written one word in the disparagement

of my sometime friend, that was not absolutely required for my own justification.* I still say of
him, as the great Saint said of the greater Sectary,
" I loved thee once ; I almost love thee still."

I have thus been, most unintentionally, involved
in the quarrels of authors; and strange it must seem,
that ever since the art of criticism was applied to
the works of " the gentle Shakespeare," the most
amiable of human beings, those works have been the
cause and source of relentless animosities among
his commentators. How grandly does the benevo-
lence and generosity of the great poet rise above the
petty bickerings of us would-be illustrators of his

---

* As my note was very short, perhaps I may be allowed to
subjoin a copy of it: it establishes how seriously anxious I was
to make amends, if I had done any wrong.

" Maidenhead, 5th Feb. 1859.

" Sir,

" I heard some time ago, and I have just seen it in
print, that you are preparing an answer to the Preface to my
Shakespeare, 6 vols. 8vo. 1858.

" If this report be true, it may be right that you should be
informed, that some months since, in consequence of what Mr. ——
said, I wrote to him, stating that if in that Preface you could
show that I had done you any injustice, however slight, I would
eagerly seize the occasion of acknowledging it, and would make
the acknowledgment public in the most effectual manner.

" With the most vivid and painful recollection of our former
and long-enduring friendship,

" I am, yours,
" J. Payne Collier."

I cannot blame the Rev. Mr. Dyce for not accepting my offer :
he might have good reasons for wishing to pursue his own course;
but surely no sufficient reason for not taking any notice of what I
wrote. He might fancy that it arose, to use Tom Nash's words,
with which the Rev. Mr. Dyce must be familiar, " out of a base-
hearted fear " of another Harvey. Not so, I can assure him.

text! For myself, I never knew that I had an enemy until I undertook to edit Shakespeare.

Of the gentleman who seems, in a manner, to have been put forward by the British Museum, to represent them in this encounter, I knew nothing until I saw his accusatory letter in *The Times* of the 2nd of July last : he, I suppose, is the literary detective of the national establishment; but I doubt how far the whole body rely upon his skill and intelligence. Perhaps, from living so entirely in the country, I never heard of him; but he has been allowed to stir up a little the stagnation of a department, where the younger men seem eager " to seize opportunities" of gaining notoriety, while the older officers have necessarily been content with the fame acquired by publication of an old chronicle, or of a venerable household-book. When first I heard that I was attacked by Mr. N. E. S. A. Hamilton, I expressed my surprise that the enterprise was entrusted to such obscure hands; and I, not very courteously perhaps, added a couplet from a satirist, which I will not repeat here, because I am anxious to avoid anything like mere personality.

From Sir Frederick Madden I was unreasonable enough to expect rather different treatment, than from a subordinate to whom I was unknown. I have been acquainted with Sir Frederick nearly ever since he was introduced into the British Museum : we have not unfrequently corresponded, we have exchanged books, and have always observed at least the ordinary civilities of life. Mr. Hamilton, somewhere in his *Inquiry*, strangely, yet strongly, reproaches me with not having lent my assistance in the investigations respecting the authenticity of the Perkins folio. I saw from the newspapers that it had reached the Manuscript Department, and I saw that consultations were held over it, not only by various officers of the establishment, but by many literary gentlemen, and especially by editors of Shakespeare, some of whose labours on the poet's works I had only heard of. I thought, not unnaturally, that if any information from me were wished, I should also have been invited to the meeting ; but not having been so invited, I apprehended that it would be the height of indelicacy, if not of presumption, in me to proffer my services, or to thrust myself into a company where my presence was not desired.

It seemed the more likely that I should have been asked to attend, because Sir F. Madden, in the preceding month of September, had written me a note, in which he expressed a wish, *propriis oculis*, to inspect the Perkins folio. The chief business of his note, I remember, was to thank me for fac-similes of the *Hamlets* of 1603 and 1604, with the distribution of which the late and the present Duke of Devonshire had entrusted me ; and to inquire whether I had seen a signature of Shakespeare on a map of some county of England, and whether I looked upon it as genuine. I answered the two last parts of Sir F. Madden's note, but I postponed that incidental portion which related to the Perkins Shakespeare, because the present Duke of Devonshire was then in Lancashire, and because I hoped that when his Grace returned to London, he would, as his noble predecessor had done, entrust me with the book, in order that I might carry it to Sir Frederick Madden at the Museum.

In the meantime, his Grace had confided to my care the very responsible task of preparing a fac-simile of the *Hamlet* of 1604; and the wish, only expressed *obiter* by the head of the Manuscript Department, I am sorry to say, escaped my memory. Sir F. Madden might surely without derogation have reminded me of his former request regarding the Perkins folio; and I never dreamed that he would take, nor do I believe now that he has taken, offence at so trifling a piece of neglect on my part, counter-balanced as it is by the fact, that of the forty copies of the fac-similes of 1603 and 1604 (for no more were struck off for each distribution) I sent two, in the Duke of Devonshire's name, to Sir F. Madden himself, and two others to the Department of Printed Books in the British Museum. His Grace had given me only general instructions upon the subject, and it was of my own free will that I addressed these rare books to Sir F. Madden, whom I had known for so many years; and who, it should seem, at that date was aiding the case against me founded upon the Perkins folio.

If, therefore, as an act of courtesy, I was not to be asked to be present, it would appear only an act of justice that I should have been required, in the very first instance, almost before the Perkins folio had been opened in the Manuscript Department, to inspect it, in order that I might be sure that it was *precisely in the same condition* as when I had presented it to the late Duke of Devonshire. Instead of that, it seems as if it had been at once handed over to the tender mercies of Mr. Hamilton, as a literary detective; and he certainly claims to have been the person who first made the discovery of the pencil-marks. He tells us that "the correspondence between certain pencil-marks in the margins, with corrections in ink [was] *first noticed by mysèlf."* He does not add when he "first noticed" them, whether anybody else was by at the time, nor how long the book had been in his possession before he communicated his discovery of the pencil-marks. All may have been meant to be conducted with perfect fairness : I will presume so ; but would it not have occurred to any impartial person, on the discovery of the mysterious pencil-marks, to have requested me at once to look at them, and to say whether I had ever observed them while the volume was mine, or while the book had been in the library of the late Duke of Devonshire? Such a course would certainly have saved an infinite deal of trouble.

However, I will not fritter away the substantial features of the case by these comparatively in-significant topics : those substantial features beyond all cavil or dispute, are, 1. That the manuscript notes were in the Perkins folio when I bought it in 1849, if not fifty years before that date;—2. That I discovered the Bridgewater House manuscripts precisely under the circumstances stated, and that the authenticity of some of them was maintained by the best judges of our day, both literary and artistic ;— 3. That the Dulwich manuscripts were in the condition I have described them at least as far back as the year 1796, as is evidenced, among other proofs, by Malone's *Inquiry* of that date;—and 4. That with regard to the Players' Petition of 1596, if it be a forgery at all, it was a forgery before I set foot inside the State Paper Office, before I commenced my researches there, and before I even knew where the Office was situated.

I ought to apologise to the reader for occupying so much of his time, but I was anxious, once for all, to go into the case as fully as my materials, after the lapse of so many years, would enable me.   *Hic arma repono.*

J. PAYNE COLLIER.

Maidenhead, 12 March, 1860.

ADDITIONAL NOTES.

Page 1.   I did not see Mr. Hamilton's Letter of the 7th inst. in the *Athenæum* until some days after my earlier sheets were at press, or I would have made some alterations in them.   I am glad to observe that he now denies the participation of his colleagues in office.   I only used the word " mouthpiece " as it is defined by Johnson, — " one who delivers the sentiments of others associated in the same design."

Page 50.   Having written to the Rev. J. Lindsay on the subject of Mrs. Alleyn's Letter, he has promptly replied that he does not remember the circumstance.   He, like me, regrets the death of John Allen, Esq., then Master of Dulwich College, who may have been the person to whom I mentioned the decayed state of the document.

Printed by G. Barclay, Castl3 St. Leicester Sq.

MESSRS. BELL AND DALDY'S

NEW AND STANDARD PUBLICATIONS.

The Library of English Worthies.

A Series of Reprints of the best Authors carefully edited and
collated with the Early Copies, and handsomely printed
by Whittingham in Octavo.

Gower's Confessio Amantis, with Life by Dr. Pauli, and a
Glossary. 3 vols. 2*l.* 2*s.* Antique calf, 3*l.* 6*s.* Only a limited
number of Copies printed.

*This important work is so scarce that it can seldom be met with even in
large libraries. It is wanting in nearly every collection of English Poetry.*

" His English Poem is here reprinted in the handsomest form which perhaps it
ever assumed, and we have seldom seen three octavo volumes bearing so inviting an
appearance. . . . . . Little was said and less known about the ' Confessio Amantis,'
until the publication of 'The History of English Poetry' in 1781. Chalmers
ventured to reprint it in his enlarged edition of the ' British Poets,' a work admirable in its design if it had not been disfigured by notoriously imperfect typography.
In this respect the volumes now before us seem almost faultless, for although we
have not had an opportunity of collating the ' Confessio Amantis ' with any manuscripts, it is obvious that the utmost pains have been taken, and that Dr. Pauli has
availed himself not only of Caxton's and Berthelet's editions, but of all accessible
written resources, including the celebrated copy in the Stafford Collection. . . . On
the whole, it has rarely been our lot to review so creditable a reproduction of any
poet."—*Athenæum.*

Bishop Butler's Analogy of Religion ; with Analytical Index,
by the Rev. Edward Steere, LL.D. 12*s.* Antique calf, 1*l.* 1*s.*

" The present edition has been furnished with an Index of the Texts of Scripture
quoted, and an Index of Words and Things considerably fuller than any hitherto
published. These and the carefulness of the typography are small things in themselves perhaps, but he who values Butler at his true worth, will value any assistance
in reading and referring to him."—*Editor's Preface.*

Bishop Jeremy Taylor's Rule and Exercises of Holy Living
and Dying. 2 vols. 1*l.* 1*s.* Antique calf, or morocco, 2*l.* 2*s.*

Herbert's Poems and Remains: with S. T. Coleridge's Notes,
and Life by Izaak Walton. Revised, with additional Notes, by Mr.
J. Yeowell. 2 vols. 1*l.* 1*s.* Antique calf, or morocco, 2*l.* 2*s.*

" On these volumes Mr. Whittingham has exercised all his typographical skill,
while Mr. Yeowell has collated the texts with the early copies, and so produced what
may now fairly be considered the Standard Edition of George Herbert's Works."
—*Notes and Queries.*

Spenser's Complete Works ; with Life, Notes, and Glossary,
by John Payne Collier, Esq. F.S.A. [*Far advanced at Press.*

Uniform with the above,

The Physical Theory of Another Life. By Isaac Taylor, Esq.
Author of the " Natural History of Enthusiasm," " Restoration of
Belief," &c. *New Edition.* 10*s.* 6*d.* Antique calf, 21*s.* Also in
small 8vo. 6*s.* Antique calf, 11*s.* 6*d.*

LONDON: 186 FLEET STREET, E.C.

Messrs. Bell and Daldy's

Now publishing, in fcp. 8vo. at 3s. 6d. or 5s. per Volume, red cloth,

The Aldine Edition of the British Poets.

The Publishers have been induced, by the scarcity and increasing value of this admired Series of the Poets, to prepare a New Edition, very carefully corrected, and improved by such additions as recent literary research has placed within their reach.

The general principle of Editing which has been adopted is *to give the entire Poems of each author in strict conformity with the Edition which received his final revision, to prefix a Memoir, and to add such notes as may be necessary to elucidate the sense of obsolete words or explain obscure allusions.* Each author will be placed in the hands of a competent editor specially acquainted with the literature and bibliography of the period.

Externally this new edition will resemble the former, but with some improvements. It will be elegantly printed by Whittingham, on toned paper manufactured expressly for it; and a highly-finished portrait of each author will be given. The Volumes will be issued at short intervals.

The *Aldine Edition of the British Poets* has hitherto been the favourite Series with the admirers of choice books, and every effort will be made to increase its claims as a comprehensive and faithful mirror of the poetic genius of the nation.

Akenside's Poetical Works, with Memoir by the Rev. A. Dyce, and additional Letters, carefully revised. *5s.* Antique calf, or morocco, 10*s.* 6*d.*

Collins's Poems, with Memoir and Notes, by W. Moy Thomas, Esq. 3*s.* 6*d.* Morocco, or antique calf, 8*s.* 6*d.*

Gray's Poetical Works, with Notes and Memoir by the Rev. John Mitford. *5s.* Morocco, or antique calf, 10*s.* 6*d.*

Shakespeare's Poems, with Memoir by the Rev. A. Dyce. *5s.* Morocco, or antique calf, 10*s.* 6*d.*

Young's Poems, with Memoir by the Rev. John Mitford, and additional Poems. 2 vols. 10*s.* Morocco, or antique calf, 1*l.* 1*s.*

Thomson's Poems, with Memoir by Sir H. Nicolas, and additional Poems; the whole very carefully revised, and the Memoir annotated by Peter Cunningham, Esq. F.S.A. 2 vols. [*In the Press.*

Kirke White's Poems, with Memoir by Sir H. Nicolas, and additional notes. Carefully revised. [*In the Press.*

Cowper's Poetical Works, including his Translations. Edited, with Memoir, by John Bruce, Esq. F.S.A. [*Preparing.*

Dryden's Poetical Works, with Memoir by the Rev. R. Hooper, F.S.A. Carefully Revised. [*Preparing.*

Parnell's Poems, with Memoir, edited by Bolton Corney, Esq. M.R.S.L. [*Preparing.*

Pope's Poetical Works, with Memoir. Edited by W. J. Thoms, Esq. F.S.A. [*Preparing.*

The Works of Gray, edited by the Rev. John Mitford. With his Correspondence with Mr. Chute and others, Journal kept at Rome, Criticism, on the Sculptures, &c. *New Edition.* 5 vols. 1*l.* 5*s.*

The Temple and other Poems. By George Herbert, with Coleridge's Notes. *New Edition.* 5*s.* Antique calf, or morocco, 10*s.* 6*d.*

Vaughan's Sacred Poems and Pious Ejaculations, with Memoir, by the Rev. H. F. Lyte. *New Edition.* 5*s.* Antique calf, or morocco, 10*s.* 6*d. Large Paper,* 7*s.* 6*d.* Antique calf, 14*s.* Antique morocco, 15*s.*

" Preserving all the piety of George Herbert, they have less of his quaint and fantastic turns, with a much larger infusion of poetic feeling and expression."—*Lyte.*

The Aldine Edition of Bishop Jeremy Taylor's Rule and Exercises of Holy Living and Holy Dying. 2*s.* 6*d.* each. Flexible morocco, 6*s.* 6*d.* each. Antique calf, 7*s.* 6*d.* each. Also in one volume, 5*s.* Antique calf, or morocco, 10*s.* 6*d.*

Bishop Butler's Analogy of Religion; with Analytical Introduction and copious Index, by the Rev. E. Steere, LL.D. 6*s.* Antique calf, 11*s.* 6*d.*

Locke on the Conduct of the Human Understanding; edited by Bolton Corney, Esq., M.R.S.L. 3*s.* 6*d.* Antique calf, 8*s.* 6*d.*

" I cannot think any parent or instructor justified in neglecting to put this little treatise into the hands of a boy about the time when the reasoning faculties become developed."—*Hallam.*

Ultimate Civilisation. By Isaac Taylor, Esq., Author of "The Physical Theory of Another Life." 6*s.*

Logic in Theology, and other Essays. By Isaac Taylor, Esq., Author of " The Physical Theory of Another Life," 6*s.*

" From the pen of one of the clearest and profoundest thinkers of the present day."—*Mansell's Bampton Lectures.*

The Physical Theory of Another Life. By Isaac Taylor, Esq., Author of the " Natural History of Enthusiasm," " Restoration of Belief," &c. *New Edition.* 6*s.* Antique calf, 11*s.* 6*d.* Also handsomely printed in 8vo. 10*s.* 6*d.* Antique calf, 21*s.*

Bacon's Essays; or, Counsels Civil and Moral, with the Wisdom of the Ancients. With References and Notes by S. W. Singer, F.S.A. 5*s.* Morocco, or antique calf, 10*s.* 6*d.*

Bacon's Novum Organum. Newly translated, with short Notes, by the Rev. Andrew Johnson, M.A. 6*s.* Antique calf, 11*s.* 6*d.*

Bacon's Advancement of Learning. Edited, with short Notes, by the Rev. G. W. Kitchin, M.A. Christ Church, Oxford. [*Preparing.*

New and Standard Poetry.

Pictorial Book of Ancient Ballad Poetry of Great Britain, Historical, Traditional, and Romantic: together with a Selection of Modern Imitations, and some Translations, with Introductory Notes and Glossary, &c. Edited by J. S. Moore. *New and Improved Edition.* 8vo. Half-bound, 14s. Antique morocco, 21s.

Nightingale Valley: a Collection of the Choicest Lyrics and Short Poems in the English Language. Edited by Giraldus. Fcap. 8vo. 5s. Antique morocco, 10s. 6d.

Day and Night Songs and The Music Master, a Love Poem. By William Allingham. With Nine Woodcuts. Fcap. 6s. 6d.

Legends and Lyrics, by Adelaide Anne Proctor. *Fourth Edition.* Fcap. 8vo. 5s. Antique or best plain morocco, 10s. 6d.

The Legend of the Golden Prayers, and other Poems. By C. F. Alexander, Author of " Moral Songs," " Verses for Holy Seasons," &c. Fcap. 8vo. 5s. Morocco, 10s. 6d.

Verses for Holy Seasons. By the same Author. Edited by the Very Rev. W. F. Hook, D.D. *Fourth Edition.* Fcap. 3s. 6d. Morocco, 8s. 6d.

Passion Week: A Collection of Poetical Pieces on Subjects suited to that Holy Season. Compiled by E. M. Townsend, Editor of "Christmas Tyde." With Sixteen Illustrations from Albert Durer. Imperial 16mo. antique cloth, 7s. 6d.; antique morocco, 14s.

A Garland from the Parables. By the Rev. W. Edensor Littlewood, B.A., late Scholar of Pembroke College, Cambridge. Fcap. 8vo. 2s. 6d.

Footpaths between Two Worlds, and other Poems. By Patrick Scott. Post 8vo. 6s.

Poems. By Thomas Ashe. Fcap. 8vo. 5s.

" There are elements of real poetry in this volume, which cannot fail to ensure it a favourable reception. The imagery and diction are of a lofty order, combining much depth of feeling with great power of expression and refinement of thought."— *St. James's Chronicle.*

Io in Egypt, and other Poems. By R. Garnett. Fcap. 8vo. 5s.

" Mr. Garnett writes with classic propriety and elevation, and his volume of poems will secure him respect, and with a superior class of readers."— *Leader.*

The Defence of Guenevere, and other Poems. By William Morris. Fcap. 8vo. 5s.

" Mr. Morris is an exquisite and original genius; a poet whom poets will love."— *Literary Gazette.*

Ballads and Lays, Illustrative of Events in Early English History. By the Rev. F. W. Mant, Vicar of Sanford and Tottington. Fcap. 8vo. 5s.

David Mallet's Poems. With Notes and Illustrations by F. Dinsdale, LL.D., F.S.A. *New Edition.* Post 8vo. 10s. 6d.

Percy's Reliques of Ancient English Poetry. 3 vols. sm. 8vo. 15s. Half-bound, 18s. Antique calf, or morocco, 1l. 11s. 6d.

Ellis's Specimens of Early English Poetry. 3 vols. sm. 8vo. 15s. Half-bound, 18s. Antique calf, or morocco, 1l. 11s. 6d.

Ballads and Songs of Yorkshire. Edited by C. J. D. Ingledew.
[*In the press.*]

LONDON: BELL AND DALDY, 186 FLEET STREET, E.C.